Home Office Research Study 215

Linking Serious Sexual Assaults Through Behaviour

Don Grubin
Peter Kelly
Chris Brunsdon

"The views expressed in this report are those of the authors, not necessarily those of the Home Office (nor do they reflect Government policy)."

Home Office
Research, Development and Statistics Directorate

Home Office Research Studies

The Home Office Research Studies are reports on research undertaken by or on behalf of the Home Office. They cover the range of subjects for which the Home Secretary has responsibility. Titles in the series are listed at the back of this report (copies are available from the address on the back cover). Other publications produced by the Research, Development and Statistics Directorate include Research Findings, the Research Bulletin, Statistical Bulletins and Statistical Papers.

The Research, Development and Statistics Directorate

RDS is part of the Home Office. The Home Office's purpose is to build a safe, just and tolerant society in which the rights and responsibilities of individuals, families and communities are properly balanced and the protection and security of the public are maintained.

RDS is also a part of the Government Statistical Service (GSS). One of the GSS aims is to inform Parliament and the citizen about the state of the nation and provide a window on the work and performance of government, allowing the impact of government policies and actions to be assessed.

Therefore -

Research Development and Statistics Directorate exists to improve policy making, decision taking and practice in support of the Home Office purpose and aims, to provide the public and Parliament with information necessary for informed debate and to publish information for future use.

First published 2001
Application for reproduction should be made to the Communications and Development Unit, Room 201, Home Office, 50 Queen Anne's Gate, London SW1H 9AT.

ISBN 1 84082 560 X
ISSN 0072 6435

Foreword

Recognition that a single offender has committed a number of serious crimes is relatively straightforward if forensic and physical evidence exists. When, or before, such evidence is unavailable, however, analysis of offence behaviour may be used to identify a linked series of crimes. This report describes a study that examined the extent to which behavioural consistency is a regular feature of serial sex offending against females unknown to their attackers. The study explored how this might be used systematically to support the linking of crimes. The research developed a method of analysis based on the routine and systematic comparison of serious offences, selecting cases on the basis of their behavioural similarity that are appropriate for more detailed attention by detectives and crime analysts.

The report will be useful to practitioners involved in crime linking and will be of interest to all those involved in serious crime investigations.

Carole F. Willis
Head of the Policing and Reducing Crime Unit
Research, Development and Statistics Directorate
Home Office.
2001

Acknowledgements

The current work has been conducted as part of the Policing and Reducing Crime Unit (PRCU) serious crime research programme. In its efforts to respond to the operational issues facing crime investigators, the programme receives valued support and contributions from the staff of the National Crime Faculty (NCF) at the Police Staff College, Bramshill.

The database on which this project is based was compiled by Mrs Anne Davies while she was seconded to the former Police Research Group from the Metropolitan Police. The amount of work and thought this involved cannot be overestimated, and we are grateful to her for a job well done. In addition both she and Mr Dick Oldfield of the Policing and Reducing Crime Unit provided invaluable input into the conceptualisation and continued development of the project, without which things would have stalled very early on. Similarly, without the backbreaking statistical work carried out by Dr Salma Ayis in Year 1 life would have been very much more difficult for us in Years 2 and 3. We would also like to thank the Royal Canadian Mounted Police for making ViCLAS available to us. Finally, thanks go to Dick Oldfield and Nicky Smith (PRCU) who provided guidance and comments on the initial drafts of this report.

The authors

Don Grubin is a Professor of Forensic Psychiatry at the University of Newcastle.

Peter Kelly is Director of Health of the Medical Research Centre at the University of Teeside.

Chris Brunsdon is a Lecturer for the Department of Town and Country Planning at the University of Newcastle, and was on secondment for the duration of this research to the Department of Forensic Psychiatry, Newcastle University.

PRC wishes to thank Dr Sean Hammond of Broadmoor Hospital who acted as external assessor of this report.

Contents

List of Tables

List of Figures

Executive summary

Recognising that two separate rapes have been committed by one individual can lead to the development of an efficient joint investigative strategy. However, identifying linked offences is not always straightforward. Whilst objective systems exist to compare *physical* evidence, such as fingerprints and DNA, the same cannot be said for the comparison of offence *behaviours*. Indeed, it remains to be demonstrated that behaviour across offences is sufficiently consistent and distinctive to allow offences to be linked on a reliable basis. This report describes a study which examined the extent to which behavioural consistency is a regular feature of serial sex offending and explored how this might be used systematically to support the linking of crimes. Data were taken from two sources: a UK database of serial stranger sexual assaults, and a similar Canadian database.

Consistency

The study broke down each rape offence into four domains. These described the offender's behaviour in *controlling* the victim, the *sexual* behaviour, the offender's concerns about *escape*, and the personal *style* of the attacker. Using cluster analysis, each of these domains was in turn categorised into four behavioural types. For example, in the *control* domain, one of the four types of offenders appeared to be more of an opportunistic attacker who used a car, whilst another type of offender tended to be more planned, usually attacking indoors.

Every offence was categorised according to its domain types, and the offences of each serial offender were examined for their consistency. It was possible to demonstrate that serial offenders have a greater level of behavioural consistency than would be expected by chance. Of the serial offenders on the UK database, 83 per cent were consistent in at least one of the four domains throughout their series, and 26 per cent had at least two offences within their series that matched across all four domains. Although it was not possible to make a direct comparison, the results for the Canadian cases were if anything better than they were for the UK data.

On further examination, we found that serial offenders were most consistent in the *control* domain, with the same domain type occurring 68 per cent of the time in consecutive serial offences. The *style* domain was the least stable, the same domain type occurring 46 per cent of the time in consecutive offences. In terms of the evolution *between* domain types, the most striking finding was that the significant associations which emerged were not those related to one domain type evolving into another, but to domains which did **not** tend to evolve into others.

Measuring behavioural 'similarity'

An algorithm was developed to measure the behavioural 'similarity' of any two cases. For each offence in the databases, the 10 per cent of cases 'most similar' to it were identified. These were then examined to determine how many, if any, were part of the same offence series as the index offence.

With the exception of offence series of length two in the UK data set, the number of matched offences was significantly better than would be expected by chance for both databases. Performance improved as the number of cases in a series increased.

Although these results are good in statistical terms, they cannot be applied alone to the screening of large numbers of offences. While the algorithm groups offences that are part of the same series, many other offences are also included. A high false positive rate may not be a problem in a database of 100 cases, where there would be just 10 offences in the group of '10 per cent most similar' cases, but a database of 1,000 cases would leave an analyst with 100 cases to compare in detail on the chance that there was a link amongst some of them.

To reduce the false positive rate, we examined the extent to which information about *where* and *when* offences occurred could be used to filter out offences less likely to be committed by the same offender. Filters of 30km and 250 days, and of 20km and 100 days, were applied to the viable UK cases. It was found that the use of time and space filters did increase the likelihood of identifying linked cases, but by definition it risked missing linked offences that took place a long way from one another, either temporally or spatially.

Other applications of the findings

We also looked at whether offences that are part of a series differed from single offences, or indeed from the first known offence within a series. We found that some types of behaviour were indicative of an offence that is of a higher 'link potential', in particular, those designed to avoid detection (*escape*), and those in which the offender is most sexually interactive and demeaning of his victim (*sex*). These and other similar findings promise in the future to help detectives and analysts prioritise their response to individual crimes.

Conclusions and recommendations

In spite of the problems inherent in the data used in the study, the results were encouraging, both in relation to the methodology used to address offence similarity, and in respect of the understanding about offence behaviour that emerged from a consideration of offence domains. The findings of the study will contribute to the development of a screening tool to help in the identification of similar cases, but it will not provide a means of *confirming* linkage (or non-linkage) of offences.

The approach described here looked for patterns in behaviour common to large numbers of offenders rather than the idiosyncratic features of a very few serial offenders. However it is acknowledged that the latter is often useful in case linking. To be most effective, therefore, a system such as the one described here should work in tandem with a good data management system.

Finally the study recommends:

- Behavioural data from large numbers of offences are necessary if patterns are to be identified within series. Rather than accumulating massive amounts of poorly focused information, however, more benefit will flow from the reliable collection of a reduced number of variables chosen for specific reasons. We believe that it is imperative for an agreed data collection format to be developed nationally, and for this to based on principles that have been demonstrated to contribute to the successful linking of offences. Thus, these findings need to be disseminated to and considered by the Serious Crime Analysis Section (National Crime Faculty) and the Comparative Case Analysis National Users Group.
- Analysts and investigators are becoming increasingly sophisticated in comparing individual cases to identify potential links. As offence databases expand, however, the need for an effective means of screening for cases with high "link potential" will become more pressing. We recommend that the development of such screening tools should be pursued.
- In research terms, we believe that further work is needed to determine those behaviours, and the interactions between behaviours, which best link offences, and to develop the analytic processes that will enable this information to be used effectively.
- The methodology described in this report needs to be tested using the same variables but on an independent database. As it is unlikely that other existing databases will be composed of the same variables as the one used in this study, this will require a data conversion exercise.

- We had hoped to be able to explore the extent to which behavioural domains could be used to construct offender profiles. Unfortunately, offender (as opposed to offence) data in this study were insufficient for this purpose. We still believe, however, that this is a vein of still untapped potential and further research needs to be undertaken in this area.

1. Introduction

"We view means and medians as hard 'realities', and the variation that permits this calculation as a set of transient and imperfect measurements of this hidden essence. But all evolutionary biologists know that variation itself is nature's only irreducible essence. Variation is the hard reality, not a set of imperfect measures for a central tendency. Means and medians are the abstractions."

Gould, 1995

Background

Recognition that a number of serious crimes have been committed by a single perpetrator can lead to the development of efficient and productive investigative strategies. Failure to do so may delay the eventual apprehension of an offender. The identification of a linked series means that information from different crime scenes can be pooled, not only increasing the quantity and quality of evidence available to investigating officers, but also enhancing the application of various forensic procedures, ranging from the analysis of physical samples to techniques such as offender and geographic profiling. In addition, it is only when the existence of a serial offender is recognised that the risk to a community can be properly assessed, and steps taken to reduce that risk.

However, if offences committed by different individuals are *mistakenly* linked together and labelled as those of a single, serial offender, the impact on an investigation can be as powerfully negative as the correct recognition of a series is positive. The belief that a serial offender is at large not only creates a sense of urgency amongst investigators, but it also generates media interest and raises anxieties in the general public that, justified or not, have a marked impact on a community's sense of security. Resources are committed and lines of enquiry pursued in ways that can be difficult to reverse. Reaching a decision that offences are linked must clearly be taken with care.

Establishing that discrete offences are part of a series is a two stage process: first, similarities between offences need to be recognised so that the possibility of a link between them can be considered; then it needs to be demonstrated that these similarities are more than just coincidence. Neither step is straightforward. Similarities between offences may be prominent but go unnoticed, particularly when they take place over territories that cover more than one police force area, or where they occur sporadically over a lengthy period of time. When similarities are less obvious, they may simply be missed, even when offences are geographically or temporally close. These problems have been referred to as key elements of "linkage blindness" (Eggar, 1990).

In order to overcome linkage blindness, procedures such as the routine screening of all cases of a related type (for example, "stranger rape", "non-domestic murder", or "abduction") on a regional or national basis have been advocated. However, for routine screening, or indeed for any case comparison procedure, to be successful, techniques are required that will recognise reliably when similarities between cases are not simply coincidental. This necessitates:

- the identification of relevant offence features;
- a valid procedure to compare offences based on these features to determine the degree of match between them; and,
- a means to calculate the likelihood that any correspondence between cases is more than a random event.

Linkage techniques

Physical measures

The most reliable means of establishing a link between offences, particularly sexual ones, is by matching DNA samples from separate crime scenes. At the very least, this can demonstrate that an individual was present at some time at both locations.

Analytic techniques to compare samples of DNA are becoming increasingly refined, and large population base rates of DNA profiles are available, making it possible to express with precision the *likelihood* that two samples are from the same individual. In the United Kingdom, DNA analysis has reached the stage where it has been possible to establish a centralised DNA database that has already begun to decrease the incidence of linkage blindness when this type of evidence is available.

However, even this purely physical and apparently objective measure of similarity is not wholly free of controversy. Uncertainties may be introduced, for example, by variations in technique, interpretation of results, and choice of base population (Davies, 1990; Balding &

Donnelly, 1994; Redmayne, 1995). Regardless of how computerised or automated an analysis system is, human input, and hence potential error, is necessary at some stage of the procedure.

Other types of physical information may also be useful in suggesting a link between cases. Fingerprints and footprints can mark a trail leading to a single individual, as can the use by an offender of unusual accessories, such as a specific type of mask or glove, make of weapon, or a particular car. Less reliable, but relatively easy to make sense of, are witness or victim descriptions of an attacker, his accent or dialect, and in some cases his smell. It is difficult to quantify, however, how confident one should be about the degree of similarity between characteristics such as these, or the extent to which they originate from the same source (Kebbell and Wagstaff, 1999). Much depends on the distinctiveness of the described characteristic, and the extent to which similar features are described by different observers.

Although not always as straightforward as one might like, DNA and other types of physical evidence provide more or less objective ways to establish links between offences, and on the whole do not create great problems in interpretation. With the aid of computerised databases and improved communication between police forces both nationally and internationally, the ability to compare relevant pieces of information of this type is becoming increasingly possible. The challenge is to ensure that relevant information is routinely collected.

Behaviour measures

It is often the case that hard physical evidence is either absent from a crime scene, or inconclusive, and linkage must be looked for in other ways. In particular, the manner in which offences are carried out may suggest that a single perpetrator is responsible for different offences. In this respect, attention is often focused on *modus operandi,* that is, an offender's "way of working" (Davies, 1992). Research into offender behaviour carried out by the FBI Behavioral Science Unit in the 1980s, together with the application of a number of associated theoretical principles, has led to claims that many offenders leave behavioural "signatures" or "calling cards" at the scenes of their crimes which are different from their modus operandi. These signatures are said to be as distinctive as other, more concrete physical forms of evidence (Douglas & Munn, 1992a, 1992b).

Behavioural "signatures" are in effect simply behaviours that are carried out consistently across offences (although this is often a *post hoc* observation i.e. made only after it is known that a single offender is involved). When particularly unusual, such as where a specific ritual is followed, the presence of a signature may be obvious. But in the absence of a highly distinctive behaviour, there are an almost infinite number of possible behavioural variables to consider in the search for consistency, and a reliable means of identifying these key behaviours remains elusive. How then can the presence of a signature be distinguished in the midst of large amounts of less relevant and often distracting behavioural information? Indeed, how can we avoid seeing a signature that is not in fact there?

Various attempts have been made to identify key behavioural variables in stranger sexual offences (Davies, 1992; Ressler, Douglas, Burgess, & Burgess, 1992), but only limited progress has been made. Nevertheless, the ability of computers to manage large amounts of data has led to the introduction of a number of systems designed to address the issue of offence linkage. As yet there are only anecdotal accounts of success, with objective tests of efficiency still lacking. A description of some of these systems, as well as an account of more basic research underlying the search for offence linkage, can be found in Appendix A.

Unlike the matching of DNA samples where comparison parameters are well established, we have only a limited understanding of which variables to compare, and of what counts as a good match between them, when searching for relevant offence behaviours. Just as important, we do not have population base rates that will allow estimates of how frequently specific behaviours, or combinations of behaviours, occur. In the absence of such base rates it is not possible to estimate the likelihood that a particular behavioural pattern relates to a single source. Without a foundation of this sort, it is hard to see how offender behaviour can be used to establish offence linkage in more than a hit or miss manner in individual cases, while the development of reliable routine screening procedures will simply not be possible.

There is an even more fundamental problem that must be resolved before offence behaviour can be used reliably to establish offence linkage: although it is assumed that aspects of behaviour are consistent across offences, this has not in fact ever been demonstrated. Indeed, as Stephen Gould's observed, nature is characterised by variation, not uniformity. Consistency may exist always or sometimes, or it may be an artefact imposed by an eager observer. The search for a common behavioural thread linking the offences of a single individual may be like searching for a black cat in a dark room that isn't there. Behavioural consistency by offenders is something that still needs to be proved.

Aim of the project

The purpose of this project is to determine the extent to which behavioural consistency is a feature of serial offending, looking to the development of a method of analysis of offence behaviour that can contribute to the identification of linked offences of serious crime.

The focus of this report is on serious, sexually oriented crimes against females who were unknown to their attackers. The ultimate goal is to create a computer-based screening system that will allow routine and systematic comparison of serious offences on a national basis, selecting cases on the basis of their behavioural similarity that are appropriate for more detailed attention by detectives or crime analysts.

2. The Data

Introduction

Two databases were used for this study. The first comprised 470 cases of serious sexual attacks, of which 468 could be analysed; mainly rape, on adult women in England, Wales and Scotland. Offences on this database were committed between 1965 and 1993, with the majority (86%) taking place in the latter 10 years. All cases were solved, and each involved an attacker who was previously unknown to his victim. Data on these sexual attacks were collected from police documentation and coded for analysis by a Metropolitan Police Service scientist seconded to the Home Office (Mrs Anne Davies), the offences themselves having been submitted by individual forces following a request for "cases of solved stranger rape". The response rate varied between forces: while 33 sent cases, approximately 60 per cent of the offences came from five police force areas (the Metropolitan Police, West Yorkshire, Humberside, Greater Manchester, and Northumbria).

The 468 cases on the database were committed by 210 offenders, 129 of whom were convicted of a single database offence and 81 of two or more. The distribution of the number of attacks per offender is shown in Table 2.1. It can be seen that the majority of serial cases involved two or three offences, with only 31 series consisting of four or more, and just six of 10 or more. It should be noted, however, that all 468 offences represent discrete attacks, and from a statistical point of view are independent of each other.

Table 2.1: Number of database attacks per offender, UK sample

Number of attacks	Number of offenders
1	129
2	31
3	19
4	9
5	3
6	7
7	2
8	1
9	3
10	2
12	1
13	1
14	1
19	1
Total	210

The second set of data was supplied by the Royal Canadian Mounted Police from the Violent Crime Linkage Analysis System (ViCLAS database –see Appendix A). It contained 840 cases of serious sexual attacks on adult women, of which 159 were solved offences involving 93 offenders. Overall, 102 of the offences were part of a series, having been committed by 36 offenders. The distribution of attacks per offender in the ViCLAS data is illustrated in Table 2.2. As with the UK data, it can be seen that the majority of series involved only a small number of cases.

Table 2.2: Number of database attacks per offender, ViCLAS sample

Number of attacks	Number of offenders
1	57
2	21
3	8
4	2
5	2
6	3
Total	93

Initially, the methodology described in this study was developed using the UK database, and was the subject of an interim report (Grubin, Kelly & Ayis, 1997). The ViCLAS rape data were intended to be used to test this methodology on a separate and independent database, although as will be seen, our ability to do so was restricted by the limited amount of overlap in the information contained in the two databases.

Limitations of the data

There are a number of general limitations in relation to both databases that need to be recognised when considering the results of this study:

- they are neither complete nor necessarily representative samples of solved serious sexual assaults (and certainly not of all serious sexual assaults) involving stranger victims that took place over the relevant time period;
- offenders in the databases may have committed other sexual assaults that are not included. Thus, whilst offences are listed in chronological order for each offender, offenders may have committed other offences before, after, or in between those that are analysed in this study. This has clear implications in terms of understanding the evolution of behaviour over a series of offences;
- the series themselves are brief and of unequal lengths, which means that the development of patterns will be at different stages for different offenders. Any apparent consistency or variability must therefore be treated with caution; and,
- it must be assumed that each offender was in fact responsible for the offences for which he was convicted.

In addition to these general points, a number of other more specific issues must be addressed if one is to have an accurate understanding both of the data set, and of any results coming from it.

First, the data for each attack is based on information originally collected by police officers in the course of a criminal investigation. This includes evidence obtained at the scene of the attack, results of any medical examinations of the victim, and statements made by the victim. Thus, data collection was undertaken by hundreds of different individuals, whose purposes were not to create a research database but to solve serious crimes. In addition, the most important informant, the victim herself, will have been frightened and under great stress at the time of the assault, and traumatised afterwards; her observations will not be those of a detached observer. Indeed, even in the much less charged atmosphere associated with burglary, it has been found that the descriptions of offenders provided by victims, as well as the recording of these descriptions by the police, are not infrequently mistaken (Farrington & Lambert, 1992). *Thus, the quantity and quality of information recorded varies considerably from case to case, is often imprecise, and is almost certainly at times inaccurate.*

Second, in neither the UK nor the ViCLAS databases were reliability checks made on the coding of data itself, such as comparing the results when a single offence is coded on two different occasions, and it may be that the way in which information was entered varied over time. It is possible, for example, that an artificial consistency in a series may have been produced simply because offences within it were coded sequentially.

Third, there is an unlimited amount of information that could potentially be extracted from the raw accounts. Variables selected for inclusion in each of the data sets are based on the research literature and hypotheses of offence behaviour. Whether variables other than those actually used might have been more powerful for our purposes was not something that could be investigated within the remit of this project.

In summary, therefore, it needs to be emphasised that the primary data used in this project lacks the crispness one would usually prefer in a research study. While accepting that this is the reality in terms of crime data collected in a retrospective manner, the potential for error this introduces in a systematic search for consistency should not be ignored. The ways in which we dealt with these and other data problems are described in Appendix B.

3. Methodology

An overview of the problem

If behaviour is to provide a means for linking offences committed by the same individual, it must be assumed that at least some behaviours are either consistent across offences, or evolve in predictable ways. The FBI reports describe many examples where this is the case (Hazelwood, Reboussin, & Warren, 1989; Hazelwood & Warren, 1990; Ressler *et al.*, 1992), but the extent to which such consistency is a common feature amongst serial rapists has not been demonstrated. Even assuming that consistency is the rule rather than the exception, however, there remain a number of practical difficulties in developing a system that can make use of it:

- *Consistent but extremely common behaviours*: although an offender may regularly display certain behaviours in the course of his offences, so too may many other offenders – i.e. the base rate of the behaviour in the "general population" of rapists is high. The use of a threat such as, "Shut up and you won't get hurt", for example, is unlikely to discriminate between rapists.
- *Consistent, but extremely uncommon behaviours*: idiosyncratic behaviours that clearly indicate a single person is responsible for a number of offences are useful to investigating officers, but they are not easily incorporated into a generalised screen. An offender who travels to his crimes dressed as a woman or riding on a bicycle, for example, may be easily associated with a series. To capture such information routinely on a standard proforma would require a questionnaire of thousands of questions to ensure that all possibly relevant characteristics were captured, most of which would be recorded as negative; even then, new variables would almost certainly need to be added over time.
- *Variations in consistency*: although it may be the case that most offenders display consistent behaviours, different offenders may be consistent in different ways.
- *The precision of description*: it is not clear how similar behaviours need to be to each other before one counts them as the same. For example, is the key element the fact that an offender *breaks into* a house, that he approaches from *behind* the house, or that he enters through a *window*? Clearly, the more exact one is in describing behaviour, the less likely one is to observe consistency between offences.

- *Victim response*: some of what an offender does during an attack is dependent upon his victim's actions, or even on his perception of her. Davies (1992), for example, describes one rapist who was physically and verbally abusive to older and to lower social class victims, but who was accommodating and apologetic to a young middle class one.
- *The weighting of behaviours*: some behaviours may be more important than others for different offenders. Although it is theoretically possible to give more weight to some behavioural variables than to others (for example, see the AMOS system in Appendix A), at present it is difficult to see how this can be done other than on arbitrary and untested assumptions.
- *Evolution of behaviours*: the most stable of behaviours may change over time. Indeed, even the FBI acknowledge that the putative signature of a serial rapist may evolve (Douglas & Munn, 1992b). Thus, the position of two attacks within a series may have a marked impact on whether or not consistency is observed.
- *The interpretation of behaviours*: in order to correct for the vagaries caused by environment and by interaction between offender and victim, it may be necessary to interpret what a behaviour "means", and to use this explanation as the fundamental variable. For example, the extent of violence within an attack, which is influenced by a variety of external factors, may be considered less critical than the *purpose* of the violence, such as whether it was instrumental or sadistic (Warren, Reboussin, Hazelwood, & Wright, 1991). The problem, of course, is that a behaviour may mean something different to the attacker than it does to a victim, a police officer, or a researcher, and then something different again to another researcher.

Even if all these issues can be resolved, it may remain the case that genuine patterns in a database will still not be identified, either because of the volume and complexity of the data, or due to limitations in the statistical method.

The conceptual approach

Given the complexities described above and the findings of earlier research reported in Appendix A, we concluded that it would be necessary to apply multivariate techniques that allowed for objective and quantitative testing of apparent similarities between offences. Thus, rather than focusing on one or two key behaviours in isolation, we look at the ways in which a number of offence behaviours interact with each other. Our starting premise is that rape attacks can be organised into distinct types based on the way in which the different behaviours that comprise the attack group together. The underlying theory is that offences committed by the same individual are more likely to be of the same type than those committed by other offenders. The problem is in defining enough offence types to enable comparisons to be practically, rather than simply statistically, useful.

Every offence in the database is treated as a unique event. If consistent patterns of offence behaviour are reflected in the typology, then the distribution of offence types and their combinations will not be random, but will be biased by these consistencies. As new cases are added to the database and it becomes more representative of rape offences generally (in other words, as population base rates for behaviour patterns become more clear), the proportion of different offence types and combinations should eventually stabilise, making it possible to calculate the likelihood of offences being linked to each other.

As an illustration, imagine that there are six offence types, and that Type 1 occurs 20 per cent of the time (that is, one in every five offences). If offence type is random, the chances that one individual will commit two Type 1 offences in succession is 4 per cent (0.2 x 0.2). If, however, the actual frequency of Type 1-Type 1 combinations is significantly higher than this, then it can be inferred that this offence type is not distributed randomly, and that an individual has a higher probability of committing two Type 1 attacks than attacks of different types. The difficulty is, however, that this still tells us little about whether two Type 1 offences were in fact committed by a single offender.

The problem with this approach is that, although it provides a means of demonstrating consistency in a broad manner, simply breaking offences down into basic types is too crude a means to establish offence linkage. In the example given above, for instance, while it may be the case that a Type 1 offence is more likely to be linked to another Type 1 as opposed to a Type 2 offence, Type 1 offences are committed by many different offenders: in the absence of other information, just because two Type 1 offences have taken place does not mean there is a high probability that they are linked – after all, in this example Type 1 offences occur 20 per cent of the time.

In order to enhance the discriminatory power of an approach based on typologies, therefore, it is necessary to increase the number of types so that fewer individuals are contained in each. To do these we broke offences down into smaller, discrete components based on different aspects of the attack, with typologies created for each. These components, or "behavioural domains", were based on what has been suggested by previous research to be conceptually valid and robust (for example, Canter & Heritage, 1990; Hazelwood & Warren, 1990; Knight & Prentky, 1990; Davies, 1992; Ressler *et al.*, 1992), although other domains could also have been created.

In effect, we have conceptualised rape offences as being composed of three main behaviour elements: those necessary to create and maintain an environment in which the crime can take place (i.e. gaining control of a victim so that a sex attack can proceed), those relating to the sexual attack itself, and those associated with leaving the crime scene and avoiding detection. In addition, we defined a fourth aspect to the offence that, while not directly related to the three purposeful goals described above, colours the behaviours associated with them, reflecting on the personality of the individual carrying out the attack. For example, if an offender wears gloves so that he will not leave any fingerprints, this would be a behaviour associated with avoiding detection, but if the gloves also had obscene words printed on them, this latter feature would be one related to the "behaviour colouring" aspect of the attack.

Thus, four offence domains were created:

- ***Control***: behaviours directed towards gaining control of the victim, including the way in which the victim was approached and targeted, so that the sexual aspect of the attack can take place;
- ***Sex***: behaviours associated with the sexual component of the attack;
- ***Escape***: behaviours associated with leaving the crime scene or avoiding capture (some of which, such as wearing a mask or gloves, may actually relate to events that occur before the attack); and
- ***Style***: behaviours that reflect the offender's personality or offence style, but are not directly necessary for the success of the attack; many of these will be equivalent to "signature" behaviours described in the FBI research.

Based on the type of behaviour involved, each variable in the dataset can be assigned to one or another of the domains. Although this is to some extent an arbitrary process, in cases where there is uncertainty about a variable's assignment to a domain, we tested it in all domains that were potentially suitable.

Each domain can then be broken down into different types (for example, Control Type 1, Control Type 2, etc.) depending on the ways in which offence behaviours in that domain are associated with each other.

In order to determine which of the many behaviours assigned to each domain best defined that domain, and to identify types within the domains, the statistical technique of *cluster analysis* was used. The basic principle of the technique is "to allocate individuals to mutually exclusive groups such that individuals within a group are similar to one another while individuals in different groups are dissimilar" (Chatfield & Collins, 1980).

The aim of the technique is to look for common patterns that establish sensible groups, based on the way in which individual behavioural variables interact with each other. The extent to which the resulting groups are in fact useful can be tested using independent criteria. In this study the groups will be considered useful if they describe combinations of behaviours that remain consistent throughout the attacks of serial offenders.

This study did not include all offence variables contained in the databases in the cluster analysis. In particular, behavioural variables with very low incidence (i.e. recorded in less than 10% of cases) were excluded. This was to guard against the formation of clusters containing only the one or two individuals who displayed those relatively unusual behaviours. Hence, the technique developed in this study seeks to identify consistency within combinations of relatively common offence behaviours (as discussed in Appendix A, there are simpler techniques that can be used to identify the occurrence of specific unusual behaviours).

The final domain typologies are the result of repeated cluster analyses refining the variables for each domain, with those that failed to significantly distinguish cluster types from each other removed. In other words, if a variable had a fairly similar incidence in each of the cluster groups for a domain, it was judged to contribute little to the definition of the group. Overall, it was found that four cluster types for each domain gave the best results.

Once types are established by the cluster analysis, it can be a useful exercise to attempt to conceptualise the "meaning" of the cluster, that is, to explore whether there appears to be a coherent theme to the variables within a cluster. Indeed, if the clusters are able to be interpreted in this way, it can provide further confidence that they are not merely artefacts of the data analysis. An inability to do so, however, is irrelevant to the validity of the technique, which depends instead on the degree of predictive power provided by the clusters: the exercise is in effect an empirical one, its validity dependent on its efficacy, not on its heuristic value.

In summary, each offence is composed of four behavioural domains, with each domain itself broken down into four types. This produces 256 (4x4x4x4) possible ways in which the four domain types may combine with each other in an offence, a number large enough to allow for meaningful patterns to emerge.

The variables from the UK dataset tested in each domain, and the final domain variable solutions, are shown in Appendix C, while a description of the domain types themselves can be found in Chapter 4.

Overall, therefore, typologies for each domain were created using just 30 from more than 150 original variables in the database.

As mentioned above, given the large number of possible combinations of domain types, it is possible to determine the consistency with which specific combinations occur within the offences of individual serial offenders, as opposed to their frequency in the entire dataset in general. The consistency of domain type combinations – across two, three and all four domains – over the offences of an individual is referred to as *multi-domain* consistency, while the consistency within a single domain over the course of his offences is referred to as *single domain* consistency (Figure 3.1).

In the example illustrated in Figure 3.1, the domain typology for 3 offences committed by a single offender is shown. In this case, the offender displays complete single domain consistency for two of the domains (control and escape), and full multi-domain consistency between offences 1 and 3.

The issue to be explored is whether serial offenders do in fact show greater multi-domain and single domain consistency than would be expected by chance. If they do, it then remains to be seen whether this behavioural consistency can be used to link the offences committed by a single individual.

Figure 3.1: Multi-domain and single domain consistency

	Single domain consistency			
	Control	Sex	Escape	Style
Offence 1	1	4	3	1
Offence 2	1	2	3	2
Offence 3	1	4	3	1

Multi-domain consistency

Summary of key features of the approach

- It is based upon the interactions of a number of offender behavioural characteristics rather than on one or two key variables that, if absent or undetected, could mean that linkage is missed.
- It contains a large number of possible outcomes – 256 possible combinations in the matrix of domain types – allowing for a more subtle discrimination of behavioural patterns.
- It is empirically driven. The assignment of ambiguous variables to domains, the domain typologies, and the optimal number of types per domain are determined by trial and error. This means, of course, that the extent to which these characteristics are purely a function of a particular database will need to be tested on independent samples.
- Probabilities of offence linkage are based on the frequencies of observed domain types, and of their various combinations.

4. Results: UK database

The four domains

Based on the methodology described in Chapter 3 each offence in the database was in effect given a four-part code (e.g. Control Type 2, Sex Type 1, Escape Type 2, Style Type 4). This was calculated by computer from 30 variables using the cluster analysis-based algorithm created for the project. It is important to note that because the domain types are dependent on the ways in which a number of variables interact, a single variable may occur in a number of different domain types. For example, in Table 4.2 it can be seen that fellatio occurs in all the sex type 4 offences, 80 per cent of the sex type 2, 11 per cent of the sex type 3, and none of the sex type 1; however, although fellatio is a frequent behaviour in respect of both sex type 2 and sex type 4 offences, actual ejaculation into the victim's mouth is common in the former (60%) but rare in the latter (3%). Similarly, in the escape domains (Table 4.3), gloves are most commonly worn in escape type 4, but this behaviour also occurs in two other escape domains: in the case of escape type 4, however, as will be discussed below, a number of variables combine to form a group in which the unifying feature is an attempt to ensure a successful escape from the crime scene.

The domain types for each of the four domains are illustrated in tables 4.1 through 4.4.

Table 4.1: Control domain types (based on the frequency of offences in which the behaviour occurs in each type)

	TYPE			
	1	2	3	4
Site (indoors)	35%	9%	7%	89%
Attacker known to have a car	100%	0	0	1%
Opportunistic attack	91%	87%	88%	8%
Attacker known to be prowling	17%	54%	7%	12%
Surprise attack	2%	66%	52%	76%
Victim moved	95%	88%	68%	4%
Attacker had a weapon	38%	88%	0	57%

Table 4.2: Sex domain types (based on the frequency of offences in which the behaviour occurs in each type)

	TYPES			
	1	2	3	4
Breasts sucked	11%	32%	32%	19%
Anal or vaginal material placed in victim's mouth	0	42%	0	26%
Ejaculate in victim's mouth	0	3%	0	60%
Fellatio	0	80%	11%	100%
Penetration of any orifice	60%	100%	95%	100%
Sexual intercourse	51%	100%	89%	13%
Repeated sexual intercourse	0	48%	16%	0
Victim participation required	4%	20%	95%	41%
Victim required to strip	17%	42%	56%	49%

Table 4.3: Escape domain types (based on the frequency of offences in which the behaviour occurs in each type)

	TYPE			
	1	2	3	4
Concerned about safe departure	0	64%	82%	71%
Attacker wears gloves	0	17%	19%	67%
Attacker wears mask	0	0	18%	100%
Obvious precautions	31%	99%	100%	98%
Tells victim not to look at him	0	100%	0	62%
Destroys semen	2%	6%	6%	24%

Table 4.4: Style domain types (based on the frequency of offences in which the behaviour occurs in each type)

	TYPES			
	1	2	3	4
Announces intentions	34%	100%	71%	0
Arousal	2%	38%	88%	19%
Conversation	4%	96%	9%	85%
Money taken	3%	96%	6%	97%
Inquiring personal questions	11%	37%	51%	28%
Threat if report to police	51%	80%	78%	73%
Theft	3%	66%	4%	9%
Compliments re sex	0	19%	44%	6%

From the variable frequencies for each cluster it is possible to describe those characteristics that appear to best define each type, although it should be emphasised that these literal descriptions are only approximations of fairly complex variable interactions. It has been noted, however, that the creation of domain "themes" may be conceptually interesting in that they are distinct from the exercise of establishing consistency or eventually linking offences; even if no "reason" can be found for variables to occur together, the fact that they do is what is of relevance.

Bearing this caveat in mind, Tables 4.5 to 4.8 provide a general description of each domain type, together with the number and proportion of offences in each type. As is evident from these tables, missing information meant that not all 468 offences could be typed for each domain.

Table 4.5: Outline descriptions of the control domain types (N=458)

	Characteristics	Frequency	%
TYPE 1	Opportunistic attack, car used, victim moved, weapon may be used	58	13%
TYPE 2	Opportunistic and surprise attack, probably prowling beforehand, victim moved but car not used, weapon common	92	20%
TYPE 3	Similar to Type 2, but offender not a prowler, and no weapon involved	147	32%
TYPE 4	Planned, indoor attack, usually involving surprise, weapon often present	161	35%

Table 4.6: Outline descriptions of the sex domain types (N=467)

	Characteristics	Frequency	%
TYPE 1	Intercourse in 50% of cases, no fellatio or forced victim participation	224	48%
TYPE 2	Intercourse often repeated, fellatio (but not to ejaculation), often demeaning, victim forced to remove clothes	66	14%
TYPE 3	Victim participation demanded, victim forced to remove clothes	107	23%
TYPE 4	Intercourse unlikely, fellatio (usually ejaculation), victim forced to participate and to remove clothes, demeaning	70	15%

Table 4.7: Outline descriptions of the escape domain types (N=468)

	Characteristics	Frequency	%
TYPE 1	Unconcerned about escape	219	47%
TYPE 2	Obvious precautions, takes steps to prevent victim from seeing him	98	21%
TYPE 3	Obvious precautions, but doesn't prevent victim seeing him	109	23%
TYPE 4	Mask and gloves, destroys semen, usually does not want victim to look at him	42	9%

Table 4.8: Outline descriptions of the style domain types (N=468)

	Characteristics	Frequency	%
TYPE 1	May announce intention, no theft, little or no conversation or questions	173	37%
TYPE 2	Announces intention, theft, wants money, conversation, may have sexual theme	93	20%
TYPE 3	Inquisitive, compliments victim, no theft, strong theme	90	19%
TYPE 4	Conversation, wants money	112	24%

Attack types for serial offenders: single domain consistency

The offences committed by the serial offenders in the database were grouped together and examined to determine the extent to which their behaviours were consistent across a series for each of the domain types. To illustrate how this looks in practice, the results for the nine offenders who each committed four offences are shown in Table 4.9.

While it is possible to observe patterns in the results on a case-by-case basis, it must be remembered that observed consistencies within a series will occur by chance. Take for example, the 31 series involving two offences. If we look at the single domain consistency within these series, given the frequencies with which each domain type actually occurs, we would expect to find *by chance* nine identical pairs in the ***control domain***, 10 in the ***sex domain***, 10 in the ***escape domain***, and eight in the ***style domain***. We found, however, that the ***control domain*** contained 20 identical pairs, the ***sex domain*** eight, the ***escape domain*** 19, and the ***style domain*** 14. These results were statistically significant for the control and escape domains; statistically significant results were also found for the ***control*** and ***style*** domains in series of length three (see chapter 7 for a discussion of these findings).

As series get longer, the likelihood of observing identical domain types throughout the series for any one single domain decreases. In spite of this, significant consistency in some of the domains was noted. For example, in series consisting of five offences, all three offenders were consistent throughout the control domain, while there was one identical series in the ***style domain*** (Table 4.10).

Table 4.9: Domain types for the nine offenders who committed a series of four offences

Offender	Crime	CONTROL	SEX	ESCAPE	STYLE
2	1st	2	1	1	3
	2nd	3	1	1	3
	3rd	3	1	1	1
	4th	4	1	1	3
13	1st	2	3	3	2
	2nd	2	1	2	3
	3rd	2	3	3	4
	4th	2	2	2	2
22	1st	4	1	3	4
	2nd	4	1	1	4
	3rd	4	2	1	2
	4th	4	1	3	2
29	1st	3	1	1	1
	2nd	3	1	1	1
	3rd	3	1	1	1
	4th	3	1	2	3
46	1st	3	3	1	2
	2nd	4	1	1	2
	3rd	4	1	3	2
	4th	4	1	2	1
56	1st	3	1	1	3
	2nd	2	2	1	1
	3rd	4	2	2	4
	4th	2	1	2	4
77	1st	4	1	3	4
	2nd	*	3	2	3
	3rd	4	2	1	1
	4th	4	3	3	2
124	1st	3	2	1	2
	2nd	3	1	3	4
	3rd	3	3	3	2
	4th	1	1	1	1
206	1st	2	1	1	1
	2nd	4	3	3	4
	3rd	4	1	4	2
	4th	3	3	1	1

Table 4.10: Domain types for three series of five offences

Offender	Crime	CONTROL	SEX	ESCAPE	STYLE
3	1st	3	2	1	1
	2nd	3	1	1	1
	3rd	3	4	1	1
	4th	3	2	3	2
	5th	3	2	1	1
5	1st	2	1	2	4
	2nd	2	3	2	4
	3rd	2	1	2	4
	4th	2	1	1	4
	5th	2	1	3	4
64	1st	4	1	3	4
	2nd	4	3	1	1
	3rd	4	3	3	3
	4th	4	3	3	3
	5th	4	1	4	2

Series consisting of six offences again show strong consistency in relation to the ***control domain***, although long identical sequences occur in all of the domains (Table 4.11).

Table 4.11: Domain types for seven series of six offences

Offender	Crime	CONTROL	SEX	ESCAPE	STYLE
12	1st	4	3	3	4
	2nd	4	*	1	4
	3rd	4	3	4	4
	4th	4	3	3	4
	5th	4	1	1	1
	6th	3	2	3	4
17	1st	2	3	2	4
	2nd	*	3	2	1
	3rd	2	2	2	3
	4th	2	1	1	1
	5th	2	1	1	1
	6th	2	2	2	1
57	1st	4	1	4	2
	2nd	4	4	4	4
	3rd	2	4	4	2
	4th	4	1	3	4
	5th	4	4	4	4
	6th	4	4	4	4
58	1st	2	2	2	4
	2nd	4	2	2	4
	3rd	4	4	2	2
	4th	2	2	1	3
	5th	4	4	2	2
	6th	4	4	1	3
83	1st	4	1	2	3
	2nd	4	3	3	1
	3rd	4	1	4	2
	4th	4	1	4	3
	5th	4	3	4	3
	6th	4	3	1	2
89	1st	4	1	4	1
	2nd	2	1	1	1
	3rd	1	1	1	1
	4th	2	1	3	3
	5th	3	3	1	1
	6th	1	1	1	1
139	1st	4	1	4	2
	2nd	4	1	4	2
	3rd	4	1	4	2
	4th	4	1	4	2
	5th	4	1	4	4
	6th	4	3	4	2

- Overall, for almost every serial offender in the sample, at least one of the four domains contained an identical sequence.
- Of 50 series of length two and three, 46 (92%) were consistent throughout at least one of the domains.
- Of 31 series of length four or more, 21 (68%) were consistent throughout at least one of the domains.

Relating results across domains: multi-domain consistency

An advantage of the four-domain solution is that, in addition to examining consistency within a single domain over a series of offences, one can also consider the extent to which different domain types consistently occur together. For example, one might look at the frequency with which ***sex type 1*** attacks occur in combination with ***style type 3*** attacks, or the frequency with which ***sex type 1*** attacks occur with ***style type 3***, ***control type 2*** and ***escape type 4*** attacks. As there are four domains, each containing four types, there are 256 possible combinations that could theoretically occur. In practice, the observed frequencies of the different domain types will vary, and each of the combinations will have different probabilities of occurring.

In terms of two-way combinations, every possible pairing was examined, with expected versus observed frequencies compared. Statistically significant relationships were found for every pairing of domains. For example, in the style - sex comparison, the ***sex type 1 - style type 1*** occurred 104 times against an expected 83, ***sex type 1 - style type 3*** occurred just 26 times against an expected 43, and ***sex type 4 - style type 1*** just 16 times against an expected 26.

The three and four-way combinations are more difficult to describe, but again expected frequencies can be calculated and compared with what is observed. As with the two-way pairings, some combinations occurred more than would be expected by chance, and others less so – the combination ***style type 1***, ***control type 4*** and ***sex type 4***, for example, should be found nine times in the 468 case database, but in fact this combination did not occur at all. The most common four-domain combination was ***sex type 1 - style type 1 - control type 3 - escape type 1***, which occurred 38 times.

Even in the absence of specific probability calculations, the domain combination frequencies can provide useful information about consistency. Offender 57, for example, committed six database offences, of which three were of the combination ***sex type 4 - style type 4 - control***

type 4* - *escape type 4. These offences are the only examples of this combination in the entire database, which would clearly make him a strong suspect if another offence occurred with this domain combination. There are a number of other cases in the database in which the only observed combinations are committed by the same individual in different offences.

- Overall, 26 per cent of the serial offenders committed two or more offences within their series which matched across all four domains.

Demonstrating similarity

It has already been observed that offenders tend to show consistency in at least one of the four domains, although they can show a good deal of variation in others. However, it remains to be shown that this consistency was greater than would be expected by chance.

To address this issue, we compared domain types between pairs of offences for every offender with domain types between randomly chosen offences. It was found that for any two offences, an offender on average had two domain types that were the same for both, as opposed to an average of 1.3 identical domain types for offences picked at random. The likelihood that a difference of this magnitude would be found in the absence of behavioural consistency is less than 1 in 1,000.

Domains and offender characteristics

Given the consistency in the behavioural domains, it might be expected that certain offender characteristics might be associated with specific domain types. Unfortunately, the databases used here contained only limited offender information, and as such were insufficient to explore this issue in depth. However, from the information that was available, it was found that that offenders who were predominately ***control type 4*** (characterised by indoor, planned attacks) tended to be older, and that those who were predominately ***control type 1*** (where cars and weapons were usually involved) were less likely to have previous convictions for burglary and theft type offences. Also of interest was the finding that those who were ***style type 3*** (inquisitive, with a strong sexual theme to their talk, and no theft involved) were more likely to have a past conviction for a sexual offence (although it was still the case that only a minority of this group had a sex offence conviction). This is an area that warrants further examination.

Evolution of behaviours

Although we have demonstrated significant behavioural consistency in the serial offenders in this sample, the question arises whether some domains, or domain types, are more stable than others. In addition, when domain types change, do they do so in a regular manner – in other words, is the evolution of offence behaviour predictable?

Overall, the *control* domain was the most stable between offences, with the same domain type occurring 68 per cent of the time in two consecutive offences, while the *style* domain was least stable, the same domain type occurring 46 per cent of the time in consecutive offences (Figure 4.1).

Figure 4.1: Frequency with which the same domain type occurred in consecutive offences

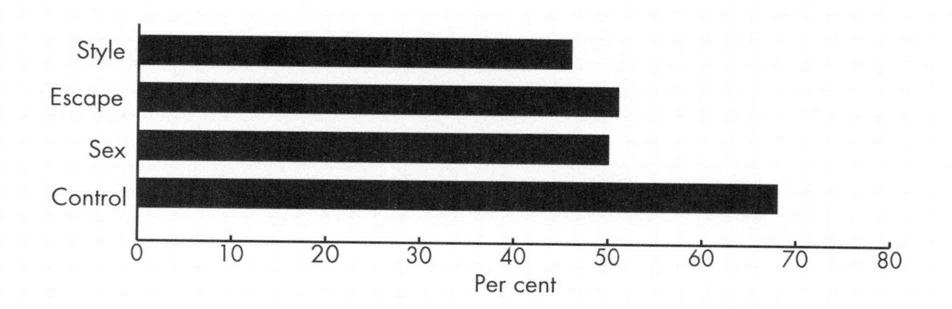

Within the domains, it was also found that some domain types are more stable than others. For example, in the *sex* domain, a ***sex type 4*** offence was followed by another ***sex type 4*** offence 61 per cent of the time, but a ***sex type 2*** offence was followed by another ***sex type 2*** offence just 30 per cent of the time. Consistency for each domain type is shown in Table 4.12.

Table 4.12: Frequency with which specific domain types occur in consecutive offences

	Type 1	Type 2	Type 3	Type 4
Control	52%	62%	63%	79%
Sex	57%	30%	39%	61%
Escape	54%	55%	34%	65%
Style	48%	37%	33%	62%

The interpretation of whether or not offenders who change across offences (in terms of domain types) do so in a regular manner is not straightforward, given the different frequencies with which the domain types themselves occur and the relatively small number of longer series. This means that the number of times domain types actually evolve is limited. For example, ***control type 4*** offences are followed by ***control type 4*** offences 79 per cent of the time (Table 4.11), ***control type 2*** 11 per cent of the time, and ***control type 3*** 11 per cent of the time. ***Control type 4*** was never followed by a ***control type 1*** offence, but ***control type 1*** offences are also the lowest occurring of the control domain types. However, none of these changes was significant at the .05 level.

Nevertheless, even taking differing frequencies into account, patterns were seen to emerge for each of the domain types. The most notable of these are listed below:

- ***Control type 4*** was never followed by ***control type 1***;
- Although ***control type 4*** was the most common control type, other control types were least likely to evolve into it;
- ***Sex type 3*** was more likely to be followed by ***sex type 4*** then would be expected by chance ($p < .05$);
- ***Sex type 4*** only infrequently evolved into ***sex type 1*** ($p < .05$), even though the latter was the most frequent of the sex domains;
- Similarly, ***escape type 2*** only infrequently evolved into ***escape type 1*** ($p < .01$), in spite of the latter being the most frequent of the escape domains;
- ***Escape type 4*** was unlikely to evolve into ***escape type 2*** ($p < .05$);
- ***Style type 4*** is rarely followed by ***style type 1*** ($p < .05$), and ***style type 3*** rarely by ***style type 4*** ($p < .05$); and
- Overall, domain types tended to evolve into those closest to them in clustering terms (see Grubin *et al*, 1997 for a more detailed discussion of the 'closeness of clusters').

In terms of the evolution between domain types, the most striking finding was that the significant associations which emerged were not related to one domain type evolving into another, but instead to domains which did **not** tend to evolve into others.

An example of evolution for the escape domain types can be found in Table 4.13.

Table 4.13: Evolution of domain types in the Escape domain. Figures represent the frequency with which one domain type evolved into another in cases where there was not consistency in the domain

	Type 1 (41% of cases)	Type 2 (24% of cases)	Type 3 (24% of cases)	Type 4 (11% of cases)
Type 1	X	32%	64%	4%
Type 2	42%	X	38%	20%
Type 3	52%	31%	X	17%
Type 4	33%	21%	45%	X

There are a number of reasons why behaviour may change over a series: it may be the result of learning by the offender; it may be due to changes in what he wants to achieve (for example, reflecting development in his fantasy life); it may have been caused by something in the environment; or, it may simply be a response to the victim's reaction to the attack. These issues are difficult to disentangle given the limited amount of information available about the offences themselves, and the fact that most series are of a relatively short length. It is something, however, that could potentially be explored in interviews with convicted serial offenders, in conjunction with the available behavioural theory in this area.

5. Results: the ViCLAS database

The ViCLAS domains

Having demonstrated a degree of behavioural consistency in the offences of serial rapists in the UK database, the intention was to test the methodology on an independent dataset. The Royal Canadian Mounted Police kindly granted permission to use data from their comprehensive ViCLAS database (described in Appendix A).

We planned to use the ViCLAS data in two ways. First, we wanted to test whether the same variables that defined the domains in the UK data would produce a similar degree of consistency across the ViCLAS offences. Unfortunately, there was not a one-to-one correspondence between variables in the two databases, and we were unable to carry out this exercise. Of the 30 variables that determined the four domains in the UK data, three ("prowling", "repeated sexual intercourse" and "expresses concern about escape") were not recorded in ViCLAS, and nine were only recorded in free text rather than routine coding, making their reliability doubtful. Overall, there was a good or exact match for only 17 of the 30 variables (54%).

However, we were able to meet our second goal, which was to repeat the entire domain formation algorithm with the ViCLAS data in order to determine those variables most relevant for this data set. Ninety-four variables and all 840 offences were entered into the analysis, using the same methodology as for the UK data. However, because there were a large number of variables with low positive frequencies, we lowered the threshold for inclusion in the analysis from an incidence of ten to five per cent.

Overall, 31 variables were entered into the ***control*** domain, 28 into the sex domain, 21 into the ***escape*** domain, and 31 into the ***style*** domain (because some variables were tested in more than one domain, these total more than 94). The final variables for each domain are listed in Table 5.1.

Table 5.1: ViCLAS domains

CONTROL	SEX
Assault at victim residence	Ejaculation on clothes
Contact and attack sites the same	Fellatio
Forced entry	No clothing removed
Initial contact in public place	Semen in body
Opportunistic victim selection	Sexual dysfunction
Overwhelming force (blitz)	Sexual intercourse
Sufficient force only (surprise)	
Use of deception	
Victim drug or alcohol impaired	
Victim familiar with contact scene	
Victim walking, jogging or cycling	

ESCAPE	STYLE
Blindfold	Attempts to reassure
Car used	Attitude changes
Mask	Contact to assault > 1 minute
No precautions	Darkness
Potential for witnesses at contact site	Drug/alcohol - offender
Release scene same as assault	Indoor contact
Release scene same as contact	Negotiation
	Odour
	Personal questions to victim
	Talks about himself
	Victim - drug user
	Victim - non-white
	Well groomed

As with the UK data, four distinct types of offence behaviour were identified for each of the four domains. These are illustrated in Tables 5.2 to 5.5 below. Because of the different variables contained in the two data sets it is not possible to compare directly these types with those found in the UK data.

Table 5.2: Outline descriptions of the ViCLAS control domain types (N=733)

	Characteristics	Frequency	%
TYPE 1	Opportunistic, con attacks with contact and assault sites usually the same	292	35%
TYPE 2	Opportunistic, con attacks, same contact andassault sites, usually a public place, victim often used drugs or alcohol	130	15%
TYPE 3	Opportunistic, victim in familiar location, jogging, walking, etc., most likely to use extreme force	181	22%
TYPE 4	Surprise attacks in victim's residence, forced entry not uncommon	130	28%

Table 5.3: Outline descriptions of the ViCLAS sex domain types (N=840)

	Characteristics	Frequency	%
TYPE 1	Sexual dysfunction, about 50% no sexual intercourse, no fellatio, type least likely to remove clothing	322	38%
TYPE 2	Sexual dysfunction but intercourse takes place, semen in body and often on clothes	88	10%
TYPE 3	Fellatio or intercourse, less likely than Type 2 to leave semen	208	25%
TYPE 4	No fellatio, no sexual dysfunction	222	26%

Table 5.4 Outline descriptions of the ViCLAS escape domain types (N=840)

	Characteristics	Frequency	%
TYPE 1	Releases from assault site (usually different from contact site), no precautions, may use car	375	45%
TYPE 2	No precautions, potential for witnesses to be present, releases from contact site	156	19%
TYPE 3	Uses car, release site usually different from contact and assault sites, precautions more likely than for Types 1 and 2	126	15%
TYPE 4	Takes precautions, contact, release and assault sites the same	183	22%

Table 5.5 Outline descriptions of the ViCLAS style domain types (N=840)

	Characteristics	Frequency	%
TYPE 1	Talkative, tends to be well groomed but may be distinctive smell, may have used alcohol or drugs, attacks indoors	163	19%
TYPE 2	Less talkative but may negotiate or reassure	219	26%
TYPE 3	Talkative but unlikely to negotiate or reassure, non-white victims, attacks outdoors and at night	151	18%
TYPE 4	Talkative but unlikely to negotiate or reassure, unlikely to display change in attitude, unlikely to have used drugs or alcohol, most likely to attack during day, delay between contact and assault	307	37%

Single domain consistency

In terms of single domain consistency, the results for the ViCLAS cases were if anything better than they were for the UK data. In series consisting of two offences, ***control*** exceeded the number of identical pairs expected by chance by a factor of 2.5 (compared with 2.2 in the UK data); 67 per cent of tow offence series contained an identical pair of ***control domain types***, compared with the expected 27 per cent. ***Escape*** exceeded the expected number by a factor of 2.3 (compared with 1.9 in the UK data), and style by a factor of 2.6 (compared with 1.8 in the UK data). Again, ***sex*** appeared to be the least consistent domain in series of length two, producing 1.7 times the expected number of identical pairs (while in the UK data there were fewer than expected identical pairs). With the exception of ***sex***, these results were statistically significant.

For the eight series of three offences, good consistency was also found, although because of the small number of series containing three offences there is a wide margin of error and one must be cautious in interpreting the results. Differences between observed and expected frequencies were statistically significant only for the ***control*** and ***escape*** domains. In the ***control domain***, 75 per cent of the three offence series were of an identical type compared with an expected 8 per cent, while for ***escape***, 63 per cent of identical triplets were observed compared with an expected 11 per cent. Overall, the observed frequencies of identical triplets exceeded the expected frequency for all four domains, ranging from a factor of 2.9 (for ***sex*** and ***style***) to a factor of 10 (for ***control***).

Given the very few series containing more than three offences there is little point in carrying out any form of statistical analysis on the results, but some general observations are worth making. In terms of the two series of length four, both offenders were consistent throughout their offences in the ***control*** domain, while offender 63 was consistent throughout his offences in three domains, ***control***, ***sex***, and ***escape*** (Table 5.6).

Table 5.6: Domain types for two series of four offences

Offender	Crime	CONTROL	SEX	ESCAPE	STYLE
52	1st	1	1	3	3
	2nd	1	3	1	3
	3rd	1	3	3	1
	4th	1	4	1	4
63	1st	4	3	4	1
	2nd	4	3	4	2
	3rd	4	3	4	2
	4th	4	3	4	4

Both of the offenders who carried out five offences were also consistent throughout their series in one domain.Offender 4 carried out five ***control type 4*** attacks, while offender 47 carried out five ***escape type 4*** attacks. In addition, the first four offences of offender 4 were style type 1, while the last four offences of offender 47 were ***control type 4*** and ***sex type 3***. Two of the three offenders who carried out six attacks were also consistent throughout their series in one domain, with offender 69 carrying out six ***control type 4*** attacks (and five ***escape type 4***), and offender 79 carrying out six ***escape type 2*** attacks (as well as five ***control type 4*** and five ***style type 4*** attacks). Only offender 92 failed to show full consistency in his series, although even here his first three attacks were ***sex type 3*** and his first four ***style type 3***.

- In summary, 35 (97%) of the 36 serial offenders were consistent throughout their offences in at least one domain.

Multi-domain consistency

Of the 29 series of length two or three, 13 (45%) were consistent in two domains, seven (29%) in three domains, and four (14%) in all four domains. Overall, 12 (33%) of the 36 serial offenders committed at least two offences for which they had identical domain types throughout.

As with the UK data, the extent to which combinations of different domains within an offence repeat themselves in the other offences of a serial offender were compared with the way in which these domain combinations are distributed throughout the database in general. Again, significant multi-domain consistency was demonstrated, with an average of 3.25 domains being the same for the offences of individuals compared with a maximum of 2.87 for offences selected randomly. This replicates the finding from the UK data that offences committed by the same offender are more likely to be composed of similar domain combinations than offences chosen randomly: in other words, serial offenders display some multi-domain as well as single domain consistency.

6. Results: Linking offences

Linking offences through consistency

While the preceding chapters have demonstrated that behavioural consistency can be described across serial sexual attacks, it remains to be seen whether this can be translated into a methodology to identify linked offences which can act as a screening procedure for offences.

The methodology developed is based on the fact that the frequency with which each of the 256 possible combinations of domain types occurs can be easily determined. This allows a probability for each combination to be calculated. If the number of cases in the database was sufficiently large, then this probability would approach the actual rate that occurs in rape generally. Unfortunately, although large for data sets of this type, both the UK and ViCLAS databases are small in relative terms; many of the 256 possible combinations simply do not occur, while random fluctuations may mean that others are over-represented. To overcome this problem, we have used a statistical "smoothing" technique to even out the "spikes" and the "gaps" in the frequency distribution (see Grubin *et al*, 1997 for details).

Because the offences committed by an individual have behavioural similarities, the ways in which domain types are combined is not random. Depending upon the frequency with which their domain types occur generally, it is possible to calculate the likelihood that any two offences were committed by a single individual compared with the likelihood that any observed domain similarities are the result of chance (i.e. that the offences were committed by different individuals).

In order to test how well this approach performs in practice, we removed serial offences from the database one at a time, recalculated the remaining domain frequencies, and then reinserted the offence as if it were a new entry. The 10 per cent of cases "closest to it" were then examined to determine how many, if any, were part of the same offence series. This was repeated for every offence in each database.

The results of this analysis are shown in Table 6.1 for the UK data set and Table 6.2 for the ViCLAS data set. The observed number of links (that is, cases within the same series that were included amongst the 10% closest cases) are compared with the number expected to occur by chance.

Table 6.1 Linking offences – UK database (a)

Series length	No. of other offences from same series that included in 10% closest cases									Total Offences
	No matches	1	2	3	4	5	6	7	8+	
2	50 (55.9)	12 (6.1)								62
3	24 (46.4)	22 (10.1)	11 (0.5)							57
4	13 (26.4)	9 (8.7)	10 0.9)	4 (0)						36
5	1 (9.9)	0 (4.3)	4 (0.7)	4 (0.1)	6 (0)					15
6	6 (25.0)	12 (13.7)	12 (2.9)	8 (0.3)	4 (0)					42
7	1 (7.5)	2 (5.0)	3 (1.3)	4 (0.2)	2 (0)	1 (0)	1 (0)			14
8	0 (3.9)	1 (3.0)	0 (1.0)	6 (0.2)	0 (0)	1 (0)				8
9	3 (11.7)	6 (10.4)	0 (3.9)	2 (0.8)	2 (0.1)	9 (0)	5 (0)			27
10	2 (7.8)	2 (7.8)	5 (3.4)	1 (0.8)	3 (0.1)	0 (0)	5 (0)	2 (0)		20
13	0 (3.7)	1 (5.0)	2 (3.0)	0 (1.1)	0 (0.2)	0 (0)	0 (0)	1 (0)	9 (0)	13
14	0 (7.2)	0 (10.5)	0 (6.8)	1 (2.7)	0 (0.7)	1 (0.1)	3 (0)	1 (0)	22 (0)	28
19	2 (2.9)	1 (5.8)	3 (5.5)	3 (3.1)	6 (1.2)	4 (0.4)				19

(a) The figures in brackets are the number of cases that would be expected to occur by chance within the 10 per cent cut-off.

For example, in Table 6.1 it can be seen that for the 57 offences that were part of series of length three, 22 had one other offence from its series included within the 10 per cent of cases "closest" to it (whereas by chance one would have expected ten to have been placed within the 10%), and 11 had both other cases from their series within the 10 per cent (compared with 0.5 expected by chance).

If we consider the 15 offences that were part of five offence series, it can be seen that 14 were matched with at least one other offence from its series, compared with the five expected by chance; just one was so dissimilar to the other four in its series according to our classification that it was not included amongst the 10 per cent of cases closest to any other offence in its series, while six had all four of the other offences in their series included within their closest 10 per cent (compared with zero expected by chance).

With the exception of two offence series in the UK data set, the differences between observed and expected findings were of statistical significance for all series lengths in both databases. Clearly, however, performance improves as the number of cases in a series increases. The ViCLAS data showed similar patterns and these are illustrated in Table 6.2.

Table 6.2: Linking offences – ViCLAS database (a)

	No. of other offences from same series that included in 10% closest cases						
Series length	No. matches	1	2	3	4	5	Total offences
2	19 (37.7)	23 (4.3)					42
3	7 (19.3)	9 (4.4)	8 (0.3)				24
4	0 (5.8)	2 (2.0)	4 (0.2)	2 (0)			8
5	0 (6.5)	3 (3.0)	1 (0.5)	6 (0)	0 (0)		10
6	1 (10.4)	3 (6.1)	7 (1.3)	0 (0.1)	6 (0.1)	1 (0)	18

(a) The figures in brackets are the number of cases that would be expected to occur by chance within the 10 per cent cut-off.

It should be emphasised that this exercise was based *only* on behavioural similarity. No account was taken of other factors that would also be considered in real investigations, such as physical descriptions of the attackers, or where and when offences occurred, that might serve to rule out some cases, or rule in others.

Although these results appear good, they are still somewhat short of what is needed if the methodology described here is to be applied successfully to the screening of large numbers of offences. This is because while the methodology is sensitive, it lacks specificity. In other words, while it brings together into a group offences that are part of the same series, many other offences are also included, even when that group is limited to just 10 per cent of the database – the false positive rate is high. This might not be a problem in a database of 100 cases, where there would be just 10 offences to shift through, but an analyst screening a database of 1000 cases on a live database would have 100 cases to compare on the chance that there was a link amongst them.

Ways in which the false positive rate can be reduced are examined below.

Using time and space to improve specificity

Once behavioural similarities have been used to reduce a dataset down to 10 per cent of its cases, temporal and geographical information can be employed to decrease numbers further. In the first instance, knowledge of when and where offences occurred may mean that it is impossible for two offences to have been committed by the same individual. For example, if two crimes take place within an hour of each other, but 300 miles apart, one can rule out linkage between them regardless of how behaviourally similar the two offences may seem. Although there were too few cases like this in our databases to influence our results, an "algorithm of impossibility" may have some relevance to real life applications.

We also looked at whether attention to time cycles might improve specificity. For instance, it is possible that linked offences are more likely to occur on the same day of the week, or on a weekday as opposed to a weekend, or during the same week in a month. However, when we compared offence pairs with random pairings of offences, none of these patterns were observed more commonly in the linked offences.

Finally, we examined whether time and space could be used as a filter to increase the likelihood of linked offences being matched to each other. Thus, if time and distance parameters can reduce the probability of some behaviourally similar but unrelated offences being matched with each other, then these cases will no longer obscure behaviourally less similar, but nonetheless linked, offences.

Sufficient data about time and place of offence was available only for 82 offences. Distance and time differences between these offences were plotted on a matrix, which demonstrated "bunching" within parameters of 30km and 250 days. This, and a more narrow band of 20km and 100 days, were therefore used as filters on the UK data to exclude comparison of offences more than this apart in space or time. (Figure 6.1).

Figure 6.1: The effect of time and distance filters on matching offences (UK data)[a]

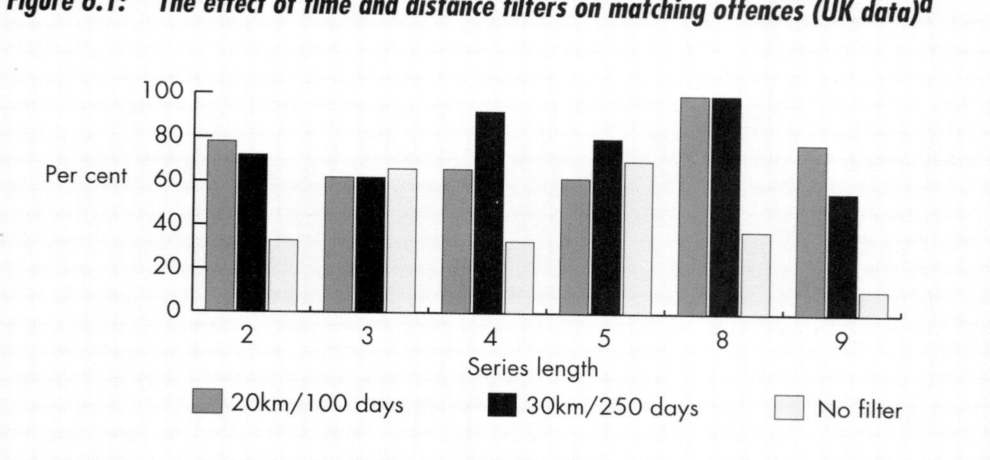

(a) Per cent matches using filters of 20km/100 days, 30km/250 days, or no filter, on all cases in the database for which sufficient information was available about the time and place of the offence.

It can be seen that both filters tend to increase the likelihood of offences being linked, particularly for the longer series. This may reflect the fact that in a relatively small sample such as this, long series committed by single individuals represent a large proportion of the offences within a specific time and space area. Nevertheless, the use of time and space filters would appear to increase the likelihood of identifying linked cases, but by definition it carries with it the risk of missing linked offences that take place at a distance from each other, either temporally or spatially. Thus, time and space filters should be able to contribute to identifying linked offences locally, but they must be used more cautiously in a national screening programme if sight is not to be lost of one of the main reasons for undertaking the analysis in the first place – the need to detect offenders who operate over wide distances, or whose offences are separated by lengthy time spans.

It would be possible to run the linking algorithm first, and then run the filter on the 10 per cent of closest cases to reduce the numbers that need to be considered. For example, using the 30 km and 250 day filter, 90 per cent of the matched offences resulting from the algorithm are excluded, while the 20 km 100 day filter excludes 95 per cent of the matched offences. However, this risks excluding linked offences, without bringing in any new ones that are less behaviourally similarly but fall within the area; in the case of the two filters, the former rejected 39 per cent of the linked offences, while the later rejected 55 per cent of them.

Advantage could be taken of the growing body of research into geographical profiling (see Appendix A for a short review) to develop more sophisticated approaches to time and distance filtering. This was, however, outside the scope of this project.

Identification of series potential

There are clear advantages in knowing whether an offence is likely to be part of a series, as this will stimulate the search for other related cases. Whether or not offences that are part of a series differ from singleton offences, or indeed from the first offence of a series, however, is unknown. We looked at this question in three ways using the UK database.

First, we performed a cluster analysis using the 30 variables that comprised the final domain types in the UK dataset, comparing the cluster distribution for singleton[1] offences and those that were the first offence in a series with that for offences that were the second or later offences in a series. In a five cluster solution, we found that one of the clusters contained 61 per cent of the single/first offences, as opposed to 42 per cent of the offences known to be part of a series. This difference was highly statistically significant, suggesting that there is a difference between offences that are part of an existing series and those that are not. However, the large proportion of cases of both types in the cluster make the distinction of little practical value.

Second, we examined whether certain domain types were over (or under) represented in the first offences of a series. We found that:

1 It should be remembered that the 'singleton' cases in the dataset are only singleton to the extent of police knowledge. The offender may have committed other assaults before or after the recorded offence.

- ***Control type 1*** was 2.3 times more likely to occur in a first offence than in a later one;
- ***Escape type 1*** was twice as likely to occur in a first offence than in a later one:
- ***Sex type 4*** was significantly less likely to occur as a first offence (and ***escape type 3*** nearly reached significance as a less likely first offence).

Third, for offenders who committed five or more offences, we looked at the extent to which domain types became more or less common as the series progressed from offence one to offence five. We found trends in the control, sex and style domains, with ***control type 1*** and ***style type 3*** becoming less common as the series progressed, and ***sex type 4*** becoming more common. However, because of the small numbers involved, these trends did not reach statistical significance. In the escape domain, the increased proportion of ***escape type 4*** amongst later offences was, however, found to be statistically significant (Figure 6.2).

These results suggest that some types of behaviour may be indicative that an offence is part of a series, in particular, behaviour clearly designed to avoid detection (***escape type 4***), and sexual behaviour in which the offender is most interactive and demeaning with his victim (***sex type 4***).

Figure 6.2: Escape domain types in offences 1, 3 and 5[a]

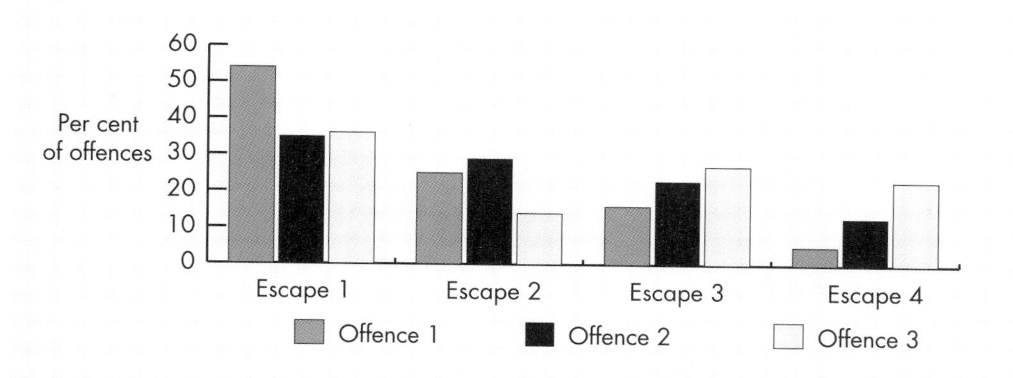

a. It can be seen that ***escape type 4*** becomes more common as the series progressed ($p<.05$).

7. Discussion and conclusions

Overview

The problems inherent in the data used in this study, described in Chapter 2, cannot be overstated. In spite of this, the results have been encouraging, both in relation to the methodology used to address offence linkage, and in respect of what emerged from a consideration of offence domains rather than overall offence types. The technique outlined here appears to combine the positive aspects of many of the approaches outlined in Appendix A.

In brief, it was found that behavioural consistencies can be demonstrated across the offences of serial sex offenders based on a small number of behavioural variables. Of 81 serial offenders in the UK database, 83 per cent had one domain for which they were always of the same type across offences (*single domain consistency*), and 26 per cent were identical across all four domains in at least two offences (*multi-domain consistency*). These findings were validated in the independent ViCLAS rape database, in which all but one of the 36 serial offenders were found to be consistent in at least one domain across offences, and a third had complete multi-domain consistency across at least two offences. Furthermore, this consistency can be used to link offences committed by the same individual.

There are a number of possible explanations for cases where consistency was not found. It is possible that consistency was lost amidst data error, or that it would have emerged if other behaviours had been included in the data set, if behaviours had been coded differently, or if series had been longer. Alternatively, environmental factors such as victim response may have influenced an offender's behaviour. Of course, it may also simply be the case that some individuals are not behaviourally consistent over the course of a series of sexual offences.

The study has conceptualised serious sexual attacks in a specific manner, comprising four behavioural domains with behavioural variables distributed accordingly. It may be that other ways of thinking about this type of offence would result in alternative domain numbers or types, and a difference in the way variables are assigned. Indeed, it may be that a more theoretical foundation to the creation of the domains, rather than the strictly empirical approach adopted in this study, would result in better performance. If so, so much the better – the key ingredient of our methodology is the use of domain types and combinations to define offences; the actual content of domains was secondary to this, and is something that can be improved upon through trial and error.

The search for consistency within domains does not, of course, imply that behaviour is static. Movement between domain types may reflect the influence of experience and increased confidence, rather than behavioural inconsistency. We have found that it is possible to identify some aspects of behavioural evolution over a series. Further research, using more and longer series, may uncover more definite patterns of domain "evolution" that could provide valuable information about whether an offender is in the early, middle or more advanced stages of a series, and which could usefully be factored in to a linking algorithm.

It is worth noting that of the four domains, ***control*** and ***escape*** appear to perform better than ***style*** and ***sex*** in terms of their single domain consistency. We believe this may be partly because the former two domains are less dependent on situational factors and on victim response than are the latter two. ***Control*** and ***escape*** behaviours are part of the "supporting structure" that allows a sex offence to take place, and as such are often pre-planned. In addition, they are also less dependent on accurate victim recall, and hence are possibly more objective and reliably recorded.

Demonstrating linkage

The methodology developed for this study requires a foundation of a large number of cases, or at least a case mix that is truly representative of serious sex offences. Indeed, the ideal database would include every relevant sex offence committed up to the index case. In the absence of large numbers or a representative sample, computed probabilities will be of varying reliability. Until the database reaches a sufficient size, expected frequencies of domain combinations will fluctuate widely as new cases are added, while the emergence of new domain combination patterns will be difficult to interpret in a database of relatively few cases. We have tried to accommodate for this statistically, but ultimately nothing will replace the need to accumulate enough cases to be able to identify patterns.

The linking algorithm produced results that, although good from an academic point of view, are as yet not robust enough to be applied routinely to the screening of large numbers of cases. Furthermore, although excluding 90 per cent of cases from a large data base may seem a productive exercise, the remaining 10 per cent may still represent a prohibitively large number of cases to sift through. In a database of 1,000, this would leave 100 cases, of which, at most, only a few will be linked. Time and space filters may help in this respect (alongside offender descriptions and other physical measures such as forensic science), but in a database of unsolved cases it can be a disheartening exercise to compare large numbers of cases with each other on the uncertain possibility that some may be linked. However, if one knew that a specific offence was likely to have been carried out by a serial offender, then the database could be searched with more purpose. Hence the importance of being able to identify behavioural clues that suggest an offence is part of a series, and having the capacity to screen for them efficiently.

Of course, serious offences are sometimes linked to each other on the basis of some unusual or idiosyncratic feature. The approach described here is not intended to recognise such characteristics – by definition it is looking for patterns common to large numbers of offenders. Indeed, very unusual behaviours are actually screened out. To be most effective, therefore, a system such as this would not stand on its own, but would work in tandem with a good data management system that can assist in the detection of single, unusual behaviours occurring in different offences.

It should be emphasised, that the system described in this report is intended to contribute to the development of a screening tool, not to provide a means of *confirming* linkage (or non-linkage). It will identify cases of interest, but it will remain to investigators and analysts to decide whether or not these cases should be treated as part of a series, based on a range of information available to them. Here an "intuitive leap", as described by Alston (1993) , sometimes has to be made. But if we are able to obtain a better understanding of why consistent patterns in offence behaviour emerge and perhaps what they mean psychologically to the offender, then the gap that needs to be crossed will begin to narrow.

Recommendations

- Behavioural data from large numbers of offences are necessary if patterns are to be identified within series. Rather than accumulating massive amounts of poorly focused information, however, more benefit will flow from the reliable collection of a reduced number of variables chosen for specific reasons. We believe that it is imperative for an agreed data collection format to be developed nationally, and for this to based on principles that have been demonstrated to contribute to the successful linking of offences. Thus, these findings need to be disseminated to and considered by the Serious Crime Analysis Section (National Crime Faculty) and the Comparative Case Analysis National Users Group.

- Analysts and investigators are becoming increasingly sophisticated in comparing individual cases to identify potential links. As offence databases expand, however, the need for an effective means of screening for cases with high "link potential" will become more pressing. We recommend that the development of such screening tools should be pursued.

- In research terms, we believe that further work is needed to determine those behaviours, and the interactions between behaviours, which best link offences, and to develop the analytic processes that will enable this information to be used effectively.

- The methodology described in this report needs to be tested using the same variables but on an independent database. As it is unlikely that other existing databases will be composed of the same variables as the one used in this study, this will require a data conversion exercise.

- We had hoped to be able to explore the extent to which behavioural domains could be used to construct offender profiles. Unfortunately, offender (as opposed to offence) data in this study were insufficient for this purpose. We still believe, however, that this is a vein of still untapped potential and further research needs to be undertaken in this area.

APPENDIX A

Review of Previous Research

Introduction

Although consideration of whether a serious offence may be part of a series is part of day-to-day police work, research in relation to offence linkage is notable for its sparseness. Much of the work that has been done has focused on descriptions of known serial offenders, designed either to develop offender typologies and assist in understanding offending behaviour, or to match offender features with crime scene characteristics along the lines of classical offender profiling (reviewed well in Warren, Reboussin, & Hazelwood, 1995). While the results of this type of work are clearly relevant to the development of methods to establish offence linkage, neither approach can be applied directly. For example, Soley, Knight, Holmes, & Cerce (1995) found that crime scene information is insufficient for the robust typing of offenders, which suggests that any methodology dependent on matching offender types to link offences will be problematic; at present, offender profiling itself lacks both the reliability and validity necessary to allow profiles from different offences to be matched with any confidence.

In addition to this more general research, a small number of studies have been published that specifically address offence linkage. This work, however, is mainly preliminary in nature and does not tend to be followed through with more detailed investigations. Samples of serial offenders have been small and biased by the way they have been collected, techniques have not been replicated on independent data sets or by other researchers, and statistical approaches have at times been questionable. Nevertheless, this work has been useful in highlighting the many conceptual problems inherent in identifying behavioural consistencies across a series of offences, and in using these to determine whether or not offences have been committed by the same individual.

ViCLAS

In North America, a number of computer systems have been developed with the aim of collating information in order to create centralised databases of offences and offenders. Examples of these include the Homicide Assessment and Lead Tracking system (HALT) in

New York, the Homicide Evaluation and Assessment Tracking system (HEAT) in New Jersey, the Homicide Investigation Tracking System (HITS) in Washington, the Indiana Criminal Apprehension Assistance Program (ICAAP), and the Iowa Sex Crimes Analysis System (ISCAS), amongst others. In spite of names suggestive of automated analytical capacity, however, these are essentially data management tools that help organise and retrieve large amounts of information. There is limited material in the public domain about how well these systems function, but from what has been written about them it is clear that, however successful they may be in *handling* data, what they do not do is perform any type of sophisticated *analysis* – that is left to the human beings who use them.

Internationally, the best known of these data handling systems is probably the Violent Crime Linkage Analysis System (ViCLAS), developed by the Royal Canadian Mounted Police. Initiated in 1991 and upgraded a number of times, its aim is to establish a database that will include a large proportion of the homicides, rapes and abductions committed in Canada, with the same information, coded in a similar manner, collected for each offence. This standardisation of data collection means that it should be possible to compare cases systematically over a range of variables. In ViCLAS, over 200 different pieces of information are recorded for each offence, covering offender and victim characteristics as well as behavioural data.

When a new case is submitted for inclusion in ViCLAS, the computer is asked by the analyst to search for other cases that may share similar characteristics, with the analyst selecting the number and type of characteristics to be examined. The computer identifies cases in which the chosen variable or variables are present, enabling the analyst to concentrate on relevant case files from which he or she can make a decision about the likelihood of offences being linked, usually based on their detective experience. It is acknowledged that this last step may involve an "intuitive leap" by the analyst (Alston, 1993).

Although systems such as ViCLAS clearly have the potential to make valuable contributions to the investigation of serious crime, and contain a tremendous amount of raw data useful for research, they are designed primarily to assist analysts work more efficiently. ViCLAS is at its best in respect of offences where unusual features are present, akin to the concept of "behavioural signatures", enabling a large number of cases across jurisdictions to be searched for characteristics suggestive of a single perpetrator. The system is not intended to carry out any preliminary screening or data sifting on its own, nor does it produce its own estimates of the likelihood of offences having been committed by a single individual. Nevertheless, ViCLAS is a powerful information management tool, and data from it has been used effectively in the research described in the main body of this report.

ViCAP and AMOS

As part of the Violent Criminal Apprehension Program (ViCAP) developed by the FBI, an automated computer search programme was established to aid in the identification of linked offences. Called the Automated Modus Operandi System (AMOS), it compares a new case with every offence already entered on its data base, looking for matches based on an analysis of about 70 offence related variables, culled from the nearly 200 variables collected by ViCAP.

AMOS sets out to achieve the best of all possible worlds by seeking to detect common patterns across offences, while also maintaining an ability to identify rare or unusual characteristics. To do this it makes use of a weighting system in which some variables are judged to be more important than others, and are scored accordingly. It is not clear how these weightings were initially derived apart from the input of experienced detectives, but from what has been published there does not seem to have been a statistical basis to the process, either in their determination or subsequent to their use.

In terms of the analysis, the total value of matches between variables is calculated, rather than the raw number of matches. Once scores are determined, the ten cases with the highest scores relative to the new submitted case are selected as being the most similar to it, and are extracted for closer attention by analysts.

Little has been published about the effectiveness of AMOS, but an internal evaluation carried out in 1990 inserted groups of two to five cases known to be related to each other into the database to test whether the system would identify them as possibly linked. It was found that the related cases were correctly matched, that is, placed in a group of ten "most similar" cases, just 27 out of 72 times. In other words, AMOS matched only 38 per cent of a set of cases that were known to be linked to each other.

This modest success rate for AMOS should perhaps not be surprising. By simply adding arbitrary weights of matched variables together, the meaning of the information was lost. In addition, it created an illusion that many different variables were being compared in a complex, interactive manner, when in reality the system appears to have been simply carrying out repeated comparisons of single variables. Both these features mean that the coincident occurrence of a small number of highly weighted variables will bias the system to suggest the presence of a link between unrelated offences, pushing real matches further away from "the top 10" and causing them to be missed. Consideration appears to have been given to modifying the weightings based on the frequency of variables in the data base (that is, taking population base rates into account in a manner analogous to DNA matching), with those occurring infrequently having a higher weight. This does not seem to have been progressed, however, and it is understood that the FBI is no longer using the AMOS algorithm.

Although AMOS did not perform as well as hoped, the idea of a systematic, automated search programme remains a good one. But if it is to be effective the theoretical starting point provided by experienced detectives must be built upon with empirical findings. Perhaps the most important lesson to be learned from AMOS is that a *combination* of police and research expertise will be needed to resolve the many complexities inherent in the attempt to identify offence linkage.

Multidimensional-scalogram analysis

In a series of Home Office reports relating to their research into offender profiling, Canter and his colleagues applied statistical methods able to manipulate a number of variables at the same time (Canter, Heritage & King-Johannessen, 1989; Canter *et al.*, 1990; Canter *et al.*, 1991). A technique called multidimensional-scalogram analysis (MSA) was used to search for similarities between cases across a set of variables relating to offence behaviours. In brief, MSA compares a pre-determined number of offence variables, and produces a spatial representation that reflects the frequency with which they occur together. Offences are therefore "profiled" in a visual format based on the extent to which a number of different variables are present or not. The assumption is that "offence styles" will be consistent across crimes, and consequently the closer two profiles are on the visual representation, the more similar they are to each other.

As an example of this approach, the group's second interim report included the results of a linkage study (Canter *et al.*, 1989). The analysis involved nine serial rapists, for whom three offences each were examined. Each of these offences was located in an abstract multi-dimensional space, but then projected onto a two-dimensional grid to help interpretation. Offences of individual offenders were connected with straight lines. It was claimed that "each of the three offences committed by the same offender occupy the same regions of space" (page 45).

Although Canter *et al* (1990) suggested that the MSA approach successfully linked together offences committed by the same person, this was not necessarily obvious on visual inspection. Many could have been more easily linked to those committed by different offenders than by the same individual. It was not immediately clear how decisions were made to group offences together, although it is understood that a correlation matrix is produced as part of the MSA process. The comparison of large numbers of cases using the visual representation would be extremely difficult, if not impossible, as the spatial field would become so cluttered as to be uninterpretable. Any system designed to be used routinely to detect offence linkage on a national scale will need to be able to deal with large numbers of offences.

It is also of interest that, although his study did not address the question of offence linkage, Heritage's (1992) results using a similar database appear to demonstrate that this approach did not reveal consistency across the offences of serial rapists. Similarly, Wilson and Canter (1997), using Smallest Space Analysis (SSA) methodology, attempted to classify rape offences according to whether their style was predominately "intimate", "aggressive", or "criminal" in nature. Although it was claimed that offenders "typically" acted within one of these styles, this was not actually supported by the results. In any case, as described in Chapter 3, identifying offences as falling into one of three types simply does not provide enough information with which to link even moderate numbers of offences.

In spite of the apparent shortcomings of the approach, Canter and colleagues have nevertheless demonstrated that there are advantages in using techniques that can manipulate more than one variable at a time, especially in relation to identifying behavioural patterns.

Fixed propensities

Another approach that makes use of techniques able to take into account the interaction of a number of variables is described in a preliminary report by Beutler, Hinton, Crago & Collier (1995). They refer to the *fixed propensities* of an individual to behave in certain ways, which is in effect another way of referring to behavioural consistency. They set out to establish whether "patterns of similarity exist that characterise the acts of specific offenders, such that these patterns can be used to distinguish one offender from another". Their study population was 23 male offenders against children.

Offenders were rated for two of their offences on a 12-dimensional scale relating to areas such as victim gender, location of offence, substance abuse, and type of force used. Profiles were then created for each offender based on the average of his ratings for each dimension over his offences. These profiles were subject to the statistical technique of cluster analysis, and the distances between profiles compared (cluster analysis is explained in more detail in Chapter 3). Two groups were identified in this way, one made up mainly of less aggressive incest offenders, the other of more aggressive child molesters.

The authors compared all 46 offences with each other in terms of their closeness across the 12 dimensions. They were able to demonstrate that the two offences of some, but not all, offenders were extremely similar. Overall, they found that pairs of offences committed by the same individual were significantly closer to each other than were randomly selected pairs, and that for any offence the one most similar to it was in fact committed by the same offender 27 per cent of the time, a frequency 8.6 times greater then would be expected by chance.

Although an interesting approach, the study was not without methodological problems. For example, non-numerical information, such as the sex of the victim or whether an offence took place indoors or outdoors, was treated as if it related to real, continuous, numbers, thereby imposing an artificial order (e.g. being male is neither greater nor less than being female). Furthermore, the detection of differences between incest and non-incest offenders in terms of the amount of aggression involved in the offence is not unexpected, but apart from this fairly crude measure, it is not clear that any other type of behavioural consistency was demonstrated.

In spite of these difficulties, the clustering techniques and distance measures used to uncover interactions between variables are interesting, and can be used as a mathematical foundation on which to base testable statements about offence similarities.

Fuzzy logic

Fuzzy logic is an analytical technique that can be useful with data sets that contain large amounts of imprecise or missing data. Austin (1996), in an unpublished report, explored the use of a fuzzy logic expert system to link rape offences. The data set employed, of unspecified origin, contained 88 solved stranger rapes committed by 20 serial rapists who had carried out from three to nine offences. Each offence was described by 141 variables. Twenty seven of the offences were used as test cases: each was entered into the system and compared with the remaining 87 offences to determine how closely it matched the other rapes on the data base, both those committed by the same individual as well as offences committed by other offenders. A "match table" was then produced that listed offences most similar to the test offence in descending order based on their "percentage of similarity".

Using 80 per cent similarity as a cut off, Austin (1996) claimed "very encouraging" and "very exciting" results, with 63 per cent of tests including all other rapes in the series above the 80 per cent threshold, and 70 per cent of tests producing a related rape as the top percentage score.

Although on initial examination these results appear promising, closer inspection of the report suggests that caution is needed in their interpretation. First, while most of the tests produced matches above the 80 per cent similarity threshold, large numbers of unrelated offences also exceeded this threshold: over the 27 tests, the mean number of offences scoring above 80 per cent similarity was 37 (42%) and the median 38 (43%). In only five tests was the proportion of offences scoring above 80 per cent similarity below 20 per cent of the data base; while one test produced just a single offence (a linked one) above the cut off, another resulted in 78 per cent of the database cases scoring above the threshold. As it stands the system does not appear to discriminate well between linked and unlinked offences, leaving too many in the pot.

Perhaps more important in terms of being able to access the approach objectively, the report contains little information about the methodology itself. In particular, the variables used to compare offences are not described on the grounds that the author has "a policy of not giving too much away to criminals about the profiling process, as they may use such information to evade identification". This means that it is not possible to determine the extent to which one or two key variables may account for most of the discriminating power of the technique. Without more information a full consideration of the methodology is not possible. Nevertheless, there may be potential in exploring further the applicability of the technique more generally to offence linkage, perhaps in combination with other theoretical approaches, for example, self-organising models or neural network systems.

Other approaches

The studies described above appear to represent the extent of the English research literature on linking offences through behaviour. However, it is worth mentioning related work that may uncover patterns inherent in serial offences that could prove relevant in the future. In particular, the dynamics of speech, and the ways in which offenders communicate their demands to their victims, may prove sufficiently consistent to allow for the creation of "speech profiles" that could help identify linked offences (Canter *et al.*, 1989; Davies, 1992; Dale, Davies, & Wei, 1996), although as yet the complexities of verbal interaction are far from being well enough understood to be applied in this way.

Geographic profiling, in which offence locations are used to make predictions about, for example, the residence of the offender (Rossmo, 1995a, 1995b), may also contribute to offence linkage. Early attempts to do this have already been made in relation to arson (Icove & Crisman, 1975), albeit with limited success. What this work does highlight, however, is the need for large and reliable databases in order to carry out research of this type.

Conclusion

A number of approaches have been applied to the problem of identifying linked offences through a search for behavioural consistency. At present, however, neither theoretical nor empirical frameworks have been clearly established. There remains a lack of testable models, and as yet it is difficult to do better than the experientially based, intuitive, often unarticulated, and it must be said, frequently successful approaches of many crime analysts.

APPENDIX B

Conventions to deal with data problems

Introduction

Missing data

One consequence of the way in which the data were collected is that large amounts of missing data are inevitable, substantially weakening the power of any statistical analysis. Data may be missing from a statement because a question was not asked, a question was asked but the respondent did not know the answer, or a question was asked and an answer given, but was not thought important enough to record (which was less of an issue with ViCLAS where a standard data collection tool was used). In order to avoid losing large numbers of cases, therefore, we used the following conventions in dealing with missing data:

- In cases where the information sought was fairly specific and distinctive, such as whether an offender smoked a cigarette during an attack, we assumed that it would be reasonable to interpret missing information as "no".
- In cases where missing information was of a less distinctive character, we attempted to amend the question in such a way that an assumption of a negative response could be more safely made. For example, the question, "*were there indications that the offender had drunk alcohol?*" was modified to, "*was the attacker under the influence of alcohol?*" in the belief that when this was positive the response was likely to be recognised and recorded. The downside to this is that positive responses to the former question are not equivalent to positive responses to the latter, but nevertheless we feel this provides a reasonable estimate of the relevance, in this example, of alcohol to an offence.

Creating dichotomous variables

As noted in Chapter 3, the way in which the data were analysed meant that all variables needed to be dichotomous ("yes" or "no") in type. Fortunately, this was the case for the majority of variables in the databases. A small number, however, such as "site of attack", had more than two possible values. In such cases, responses were merged so that they could be represented as "yes" or "no" – for example, the eight possible values for "site of attack" were reduced to *indoors* vs. *outdoors*, and *victim's home* vs. *elsewhere*.

Other variables were clearly linked to each other. This was the case, for example, in relation to *attempted fellatio, fellatio*, and *repeated fellatio*. Such variables were collapsed into a single variable and scored 'yes' if the answer to any one was positive.

While these conventions may have led to faulty assumptions in individual cases, given the limitations of the data we do not believe that they added significantly to the error already inherent in the dataset.

APPENDIX C

Domain variables for UK data sets

Variables tested for the Control domain, and those included in the final domain

INITIAL UK VARIABLES		FINAL VARIABLES
1 Physical abuse (instrumental)		1 Site of approach (indoors/outdoors)
2 Site of approach (indoors/outdoors)		2 Car used during offence
3 Asphyxiation (instrumental)		3 Clear indications of opportunism
4 Blindfolded		4 Prowling
5 Blitz attack	→	5 Surprise attack
6 Number of blows		6 Victim moved between approach and attack
7 Car used during offence		7 Weapon
8 Victim put in fear		
9 Victim cut		
10 Victim's clothing damaged		
11 Gag		
12 Hail of blows, no obvious reason		
13 Hail of blows, no interval in response to resistance		
14 Ligature		
15 Clear indications of opportunism		
16 Victim known to be a prostitute		
17 Prowling		
18 Knife against skin as part of threat		
19 Surprise attack		
20 Target		
21 Ankles or wrists tied		
22 Time of approach		
23 Two or more blows to control		
24 Victim moved between approach and attack		
25 Weapon		

Variables tested for the Sex domain, and those included in the final domain

INITIAL UK VARIABLES		FINAL VARIABLES
1 Abuse		1 Breasts sucked
2 Gratuitous abuse		2 Vaginal or anal material passed to mouth
3 Buggery		3 Ejaculates in mouth
4 Requests intercourse		4 Fellatio
5 Requests buggery	→	5 Penetr. of any orifice
6 Asphyxiation gratuitous		6 Sexual intercourse
7 Attempted buggery		7 Repeated s.i.
8 Attempted cunnilingus		8 Victim asked to undress
9 Attempted fellatio		9 Victim made to respond
10 Kiss		
11 Breasts fondled		
12 Breasts sucked		
13 Compliments re sex		
14 Cunnilingus		
15 Deliberate damage to victim's clothing		
16 Vaginal or anal material passed to mouth by penis		
17 Erectile insufficiency		
18 Ejaculation outside an orifice		
19 Ejaculates in mouth		
20 Fellatio		
21 Finger in vagina		
22 French kiss		
23 Foreign object in anus		
24 Foreign object in vagina		
25 Finger near vagina		
26 Kiss		
27 Offender masturbates himself		
28 Offender removes some of victim's clothing		
29 Penetration of any orifice		
30 Premature ejaculation		
31 Sexual intercourse		
32 Sexual intercourse from behind		
33 Sexual intercourse more than once (repeated s.i.)		
34 Sexual intercourse from rear more than once		
35 Victim asked to undress		
36 Unusual sexual act		
37 Victim bitten		
38 Victim made to masturbate offender		
39 Victim made to fondle or masturbate herself		
40 Victim required to respond		

Variables tested for the Escape domain, and those included in the final domain

INITIAL UK VARIABLES		FINAL VARIABLES
1 Condom used to avoid leaving evidence		1 Concern about escape
2 Asks for date to continue contact		2 Gloves
3 Concern about safe escape		3 Mask
4 Destroys semen		4 Obv. precautions
5 Concern about fingerprints		5 Tells victim not to look at him
6 Gloves	→	6 Destroys semen*
7 Threat not to report (personal)		
8 Mask		
9 Obvious precautions		
10 Indicates familiarity with police methods		
11 Acknowledges victim might report		
12 Remorse		
13 Threats to prevent victim reporting		
14 Reassurance/threat to prevent reporting		
15 Tells victim not to look at him		

* At a late stage it was discovered that the variable "destroys semen" had a frequency of 5.7 per cent, and thus should not have been included as a final variable. Future work will need to evaluate the effect of this oversight.

Variables tested for the Style domain, and those included in the final domain

INITIAL UK VARIABLES		FINAL VARIABLES
1 Affection shown		1 Announces what will do next
2 Alcohol		2 Sexual arousal themes
3 Announces what will do next		3 Compliments re sex
4 Arguing		4 Conversation re theft
5 Sexual arousal themes	→	5 Inquisitive, nonsexual
6 Boasting		6 Money taken
7 Compliment during con		7 Theft
8 Con		8 Threats made
9 Consideration		
10 Continues with date request		
11 Compliments re sex		
12 Conversation re theft		
13 Drugs		
14 Offender says enjoys offence		
15 Mention of victim enjoying		
16 Excuses/justification		
17 Asks about victim's interests		
18 Inquisitive nonsexual		
19 Lies about intention to rape		
20 Lies to mislead		
21 Limitation announcement		
22 Requests or takes money		
23 Compromises		
24 Insistant		
25 Mentions his penis		
26 Mentions the pill		
27 Reassances given		
28 Remorse		
29 Indirect threats		
30 Threats if reports		
31 Mention of victim's previous sexual experience		
32 Smoked during offence		
33 Discussion re victim's husband or boyfriend		
34 Souvenir taken		
35 Swore		
36 Sad tales		
37 Theft		
38 Threats		
39 Obvious interest in underwear		
40 Victim's body discussed		
41 Remarks indicating concern re interuption		
42 Virginity mentioned		
43 Victim bitten		
44 Asks about victim's job		

References

Alston, J. D. (1993). Violent Crime Analysis Unit: An informal assessment. Unpublished Internal Royal Canadian Mounted Police document.

Austin, V. (1996). An Investigation into Offender Profiling: Assessing the Performance of Automated Profiling for Criminal Identification, using Fuzzy Logic. Unpublished, Bournemouth University.

Balding, D. J. & Donnelly, P. (1994). 'The prosecutor's fallacy and DNA evidence'. *Criminal Law Review*, 711-721.

Beutler, L. E., Hinton, R. M., Crago, M., & Collier, S. (1995). 'Evaluation of "fixed propensities" to commit sexual offenses – A preliminary report'. *Criminal Justice and Behavior*, 22, 284-294.

Canter, D., Heritage, R., & King-Johannessen, K. (1989). Offender profiling: Second Interim Report to the Home Office. Unpublished Home Office Report.

Canter, D., & Heritage, R. (1990). 'A multivariate model of sexual offence behaviour: Developments in offender profiling'. *Journal of Forensic Psychiatry*, 1, 185-217.

Canter, D., Heritage, R., Davies, A., Holden, R., Kirby, S., Hancock, C., John, E., King-Johannessen, K., & McGinley, J. (1990). Developments in Offender Profiling. Unpublished final report to the Home Office.

Canter, D., Heritage, R., Wilson, M., Davies, A., Kirby, S., Holden, R., McGinley, J., Hughes, H., Larkin, P., Martin, L., Tsang, E., Vaughan, G., & Donald, I. (1991). A Facet Approach to Offender Profiling, Volume 1. Unpublished final report to the Home Office.

Chatfield, C., & Collins, A. J. (1980). *Introduction to Multivariate Analysis.* London: Chapman and Hall.

Dale, A., Davies, A., & Wei, L. (1997). 'Developing a typology of rapists' speech'. *Journal of Pragmatics*, 27, 653-669.

Davies, A. (1990). 'The use of DNA profiling and behavioural science in the investigation of sexual offences'. *Medicine, Science and the Law*, 31, 95-101.

Davies, A. (1992). 'Rapists' behaviour: A three aspect model as a basis for analysis and the identification of serial crime'. *Forensic Science International*, 55, 173-194.

Douglas, J. E., & Munn, C. M. (1992a). In Ressler, R. K., Douglas, J. E., .Burgess, A. W, & Burgess, A. G, eds. *Crime Classification Manual*, pp.259-268. New York: Simon & Schuster.

Douglas, J. E., & Munn, C. (1992b). 'Violent crime scene analysis: Modus operandi, signature, and staging'. *FBI Law Enforcement Bulletin*, 61, 1-10.

Egger, S. A. (1990). *Serial murder: An elusive phenomenon.* New York: Praeger.

Farrington, D. P., & Lambert, S. (1992). The feasibility of a statistical approach to offender profiling: Burglary and violence in Nottinghamshire. Home Office and Police Foundation Report (unpublished).

Gould, S. J (1995). 'The Median isn't the message'. *Discover*, June, 40-42.

Grubin, D., Kelly, P., & Ayis, S. (1997). *Linking Serious Sexual Assaults*. London: Home Office: Police Research Group.

Hazelwood, R., Reboussin, R., & Warren, J. (1989). 'Serial rape: Correlates of increased aggression and the relationship of offender pleasure to victim resistance'. *Journal of Interpersonal Violence*, 4, 65-78.

Hazelwood, R., & Warren, J. (1990). 'The criminal behavior of the serial rapist'. *FBI Law Enforcement Bulletin*, 11-17.

Heritage, R. (1992). Facets of Sexual Assault: First Steps in Investigative Classifications. University of Surrey: M.Phil. Thesis (unpublished).

Icove, D. J., & Crisman, H. J., (1975). 'Application of pattern recognition in arson investigation'. *Fire Technology*, 11, 35-41.

Kebbell, M.R. and Wagstaff, G.F. (1999). *Face value? Evaluating the Accuracy of Eyewitness Information.* Police Research Series, Paper 102. London:Home Office.

Knight, R. A., & Prentky, R. A. (1990). 'Classifying sexual offenders: The development and corroboration of taxonomic models'. In Marshall, W. L., Laws, D. R., & Barbaree, H. R., eds. *Handbook of Sexual Assault.* New York: Plenum.

Redmayne, M. (1995). 'Doubts and burdens: DNA evidence, probability and the courts'. *Criminal Law Review,* 464-482.

Ressler, R. K., Douglas, J. E., Burgess, A. W., & Burgess, A. G. (1992). *Crime Classification Manual.* New York: Simon & Schuster.

Rossmo, D. K. (1995a). 'Place, space, and police investigations: Hunting serial violent criminals'. In Eck, J. E. & Weisburd, D. A. eds. *Crime Prevention Studies,* 4, 219-237. Monsey NY: Criminal Justice Press.

Rossmo, D. K. (1995b). Geographic profiling: Target patterns of serial murderers. Simon Fraser University: Ph.D. dissertation (unpublished).

Soley, B., Knight, R., Holmes, K., & Cerce, D. (1995). Predicting MTC:R3 rapist types from crime scene variables. In Warren, J., Reboussin, R. & Hazelwood, R. R., The geographic and temporal sequencing of serial rape. Report for the National Institute of Justice (unpublished).

Warren, J., Reboussin, R., Hazelwood, R., & Wright, J. (1991). 'Prediction of rape type and violence from verbal, physical and sexual scales'. *Journal of Interpersonal Violence,* 6, 55-67.

Warren, J., Reboussin, R., & Hazelwood, R. R. (1995). The geographic and temporal sequencing of serial rape. Report for the National Institute of Justice (unpublished).

Wilson, M and Canter, D. (1997). The Management of Investigative Decision Making. Final Report to the ESRC (unpublished).

RDS Publications

Requests for Publications

Copies of our publications and a list of those currently available may be obtained from:

Home Office
Research, Development and Statistics Directorate
Communications Development Unit
Room 201, Home Office
50 Queen Anne's Gate
London SW1H 9AT
Telephone: 020 7273 2084 (answerphone outside of office hours)
Facsimile: 020 7222 0211
E-mail: publications.rds@homeoffice.gsi.gov.uk

alternatively

why not visit the RDS web-site at
Internet: http://www.homeoffice.gov.uk/rds/index.htm

where many of our publications are available to be read on screen or downloaded for printing.